The Waco Siege

GREAT DISASTERS
REFORMS and RAMIFICATIONS

The Waco Siege

Marylou Morano Kjelle

CHELSEA HOUSE PUBLISHERS
Philadelphia

Frontispiece: Waco, Texas, approximately halfway between Dallas and Austin, was the location of the Mount Carmel Center.

CHELSEA HOUSE PUBLISHERS

Editor in Chief Sally Cheney
Director of Production Kim Shinners
Creative Manager Takeshi Takahashi
Manufacturing Manager Diann Grasse

Staff for THE WACO SIEGE

Assistant Editor Susan Naab
Picture Researcher Sarah Bloom
Production Assistant Jaimie Winkler
Series Designer Takeshi Takahashi
Cover Designer Keith Trego
Layout 21st Century Publishing and Communications, Inc.

First Printing

1 3 5 7 9 8 6 4 2

The Chelsea House World Wide Web address is
http://www.chelseahouse.com

Library of Congress Cataloging-in-Publication Data

Kjelle, Marylou Morano.
    The Waco siege / by Marylou Morano Kjelle.
      p. cm. — (Great disasters, reforms and ramifications)
Summary: Reviews the events leading up to federal agents'
1993 raid on the Branch Davidian compound in Waco, Texas,
the raid itself, and its aftermath.
Includes bibliographical references and index.
    ISBN 0-7910-6739-4
  1. Waco Branch Davidian Disaster, Tex., 1993—Juvenile
literature. 2. Koresh, David, 1959-1993—Juvenile literature.
3. Branch Davidians—Juvenile literature. [1. Waco Branch
Davidian Disaster, Tex.,1993. 2. Koresh, David, 1959-1993.
3. Branch Davidians.] I. Title. II. Series.
BP605.B72 K57 2002
976.4'284063—dc21
                                        2002000341

Contents

GREAT DISASTERS
REFORMS and RAMIFICATIONS

Jill McCaffrey
National Chairman
Armed Forces Emergency Services
American Red Cross

Introduction

Disasters have always been a source of fascination and awe. Tales of a great flood that nearly wipes out all life are among humanity's oldest recorded stories, dating at least from the second millennium B.C., and they appear in cultures from the Middle East to the Arctic Circle to the southernmost tip of South America and the islands of Polynesia. Typically gods are at the center of these ancient disaster tales—which is perhaps not too surprising, given the fact that the tales originated during a time when human beings were at the mercy of natural forces they did not understand.

To a great extent, we still are at the mercy of nature, as anyone who reads the newspapers or watches nightly news broadcasts can attest.

Hurricanes, earthquakes, tornados, wildfires, and floods continue to exact a heavy toll in suffering and death, despite our considerable knowledge of the workings of the physical world. If science has offered only limited protection from the consequences of natural disasters, it has in no way diminished our fascination with them. Perhaps that's because the scale and power of natural disasters force us as individuals to confront our relatively insignificant place in the physical world and remind us of the fragility and transience of our lives. Perhaps it's because we can imagine ourselves in the midst of dire circumstances and wonder how we would respond. Perhaps it's because disasters seem to bring out the best and worst instincts of humanity: altruism and selfishness, courage and cowardice, generosity and greed.

As one of the national chairmen of the American Red Cross, a humanitarian organization that provides relief for victims of disasters, I have had the privilege of seeing some of humanity's best instincts. I have witnessed communities pulling together in the face of trauma; I have seen thousands of people answer the call to help total strangers in their time of need.

Of course, helping victims after a tragedy is not the only way, or even the best way, to deal with disaster. In many cases planning and preparation can minimize damage and loss of life—or even avoid a disaster entirely. For, as history repeatedly shows, many disasters are caused not by nature but by human folly, shortsightedness, and unethical conduct. For example, when a land developer wanted to create a lake for his exclusive resort club in Pennsylvania's Allegheny Mountains in 1880, he ignored expert warnings and cut corners in reconstructing an earthen dam. On May 31, 1889, the dam gave way, unleashing 20 million tons of water on the towns below. The Johnstown Flood, the deadliest in American history, claimed more than 2,200 lives. Greed and negligence would figure prominently in the Triangle Shirtwaist Company fire in 1911. Deplorable conditions in the garment sweatshop, along with a failure to give any thought to the safety of workers, led to the tragic deaths of 146 persons. Technology outstripped wisdom only a year later, when the designers of the luxury liner *Titanic* smugly declared their state-of-the-art ship "unsinkable," seeing no need to provide lifeboat capacity for everyone onboard. On the night of April 14, 1912, more than 1,500 passengers and crew paid for this hubris with their lives after the ship collided with an iceberg and sank. But human catastrophes aren't always the unforeseen consequences of carelessness or folly. In the 1940s the leaders of Nazi Germany purposefully and systematically set out to exterminate all Jews, along with Gypsies, homosexuals, the mentally ill, and other so-called undesirables. More recently terrorists have targeted random members of society, blowing up airplanes and buildings in an effort to advance their political agendas.

The books in the GREAT DISASTERS: REFORMS AND RAMIFICATIONS series examine these and other famous disasters, natural and human made. They explain the causes of the disasters, describe in detail how events unfolded, and paint vivid portraits of the people caught up in dangerous circumstances. But these books are more than just accounts of what happened to whom and why. For they place the disasters in historical perspective, showing how people's attitudes and actions changed and detailing the steps society took in the wake of each calamity. And in the end, the most important lesson we can learn from any disaster—as well as the most fitting tribute to those who suffered and died—is how to avoid a repeat in the future.

Showtime

An armored personnel carrier is deployed from the command center at the Texas State Technical College campus in Waco in this March 1993 photo.

Few people outside of Texas had heard of the centrally located city of Waco before the raid on the Branch Davidians in the middle of the winter of 1993. Located off Interstate 35, the city is surrounded by the rich and fertile farmland of the Texas plains. Waco is named after the Hwaco (pronounced "waco") Indians, a sub-tribe of the Wichitas, and the city once served as a gateway to pioneers traveling to unsettled lands in west Texas. Modern day Waco with a population of over 200,000 is the largest city between Dallas and Houston. The Texas Rangers Hall of Fame and the Dr. Pepper Museum are two of the attractions that draw people to Waco.

Weak sunlight struggled to break through Waco's overcast sky the morning of February 28, 1993. It had rained the night before, and the air was damp and chilly. Across the United States on the East Coast, New York City was recovering from the bombing of the World Trade Center by Muslim extremists two days earlier. At Mount Carmel Center, a 77-acre ranch situated on a prairie 10 miles from the city of Waco proper, members of a religious group were preparing for a confrontation with agents of the United States government.

There were 130 people living at Mount Carmel Center on this Sunday morning. Many were women and children; a few were elderly. Two members were in Austin selling weapons at a gun show—a regular activity of some of the members. All followed the teachings and lifestyle of 33-year-old David Koresh, a slight man of medium build who made up in charisma what he lacked in physique.

Since the 1930s various offshoots of the Seventh Day Adventist Church have called Mount Carmel home. Koresh assumed leadership of his group in the late 1980s. For several weeks Koresh and the Branch Davidians had knowingly been under government surveillance. Friendly neighbors had informed the Koreshans, as they preferred to be called, that local law officials had requested permission to place recording devices on their properties. The officials suspected the residents of Mount Carmel were deploying illegal weapons. On February 27, the day before, the local daily paper, the *Waco Tribune-Herald* had printed the first installment of a seven-part series on Koresh and his followers entitled "The Sinful Messiah." Written by Mark England and Darlene McCormick, the series also related allegations of weapon stockpiling, as well as child abuse and polygamy (having more than one wife).

The United States Bureau of Alcohol, Tobacco and Firearms (ATF) is a law enforcement branch of the United States Department of the Treasury with the responsibilities of reducing violent crime, collecting revenue, and protecting the public. Agents of the ATF had prepared affidavits of probable cause to obtain an arrest warrant of Koresh and search warrants of Mount Carmel and the "Mag Bag," an auto shop rented by Branch Davidians located about two miles from the compound. In addition to weapon stockpiling, ATF suspected the Branch Davidians of converting legal semiautomatic rifles into illegal machine guns. ATF planned a surprise raid on Mount Carmel to arrest the residents and confiscate their weapons. Because a siege strategy would give Koresh and his followers the opportunity to hide evidence, between 75 and 90 heavily armed ATF agents were to execute the search and arrest warrant by launching a "dynamic entry" into the compound. The official government name for the raid was "Operation Trojan Horse;" but those agents actually participating in the operation had nicknamed it "Showtime."

ATF had originally planned the raid for Monday, March 1, but after learning the *Waco Tribune-Herald* was going to begin publishing the series on Saturday, February 27, ATF moved the raid ahead a day so as to not raise the Koreshans' suspicions, causing them to plan for a possible show of aggression.

The residents of Mount Carmel, however, had been forewarned. Earlier that morning Branch Davidian member David Jones, Koresh's brother-in-law, was returning to Mount Carmel when TV photographer, Jim Peeler, stopped him. Peeler asked Jones for directions to "Rodenville," an early name for the Mount Carmel complex and one still used by the locals.

Aware that something significant was imminent, Jones quickly returned to Mount Carmel. Along the way he encountered a station wagon carrying ATF agents dressed in combat and riot gear. At the compound, Jones alerted Koresh to the impending raid, using a long distance phone call from England as an excuse to engage him in a private conversation.

Undercover ATF Agent Robert Rodriquez, known to the Branch Davidians as Robert Gonzalez, was at the compound conversing with Koresh when Jones arrived. Posing as a college student, Gonzalez had formed a relationship with Koresh and often visited Mount Carmel for Bible studies. On the morning of February 28, the purpose of his visit was to ascertain the residents' reactions to the Saturday and Sunday *Waco Tribune-Herald* articles. Rodriquez claimed Koresh was visibly shaken by his conversation with Jones and told Rodriquez, "Neither the ATF or the National Guard will ever get me." Then he added, "They're coming, Robert. The time has come."

Suspecting Koresh had been tipped off, Rodriquez immediately left Mount Carmel to warn the ATF. He reported the information to his superior, Tactical Coordinator Charles Sarabyn, who related the information to Phil Chojnacki, the agent in charge of the raid. Rodriquez reported he did not observe Koresh distribute weapons after hearing the news and had left him reading the Bible. Rather than abort the operation, Chojnacki felt the raid could still be executed successfully if they hurried.

Lacking the element of surprise, the ATF agents now depended upon their intensive preparations for the raid. Support coordinators had been in Waco since January. Snipers had already taken up positions in the rear of Mount Carmel, about 200 yards away from the building. More than 50 agents had come to Waco the previous evening and were part of an 80-vehicle convoy presently on its way from Fort Hood, 60 miles away.

ATF had selected the mid-morning hour for the raid because it was believed the men would be unarmed and outside the complex, working in the construction pit, a 100-foot long by 15-foot deep area adjacent to the compound building. Federal agents planned to quickly arrest Koresh and take possession of the firearms. Female

From the Book of Reve-
lation, the Last Judgment
is pictured in this 1866
illustration by Gustave
Dore (1832-1883).

special agents were to keep the women and children calm
during the assault.

Koresh was a man of radical religious beliefs. He
believed the world had already entered the Period of Tribu-
lation (preceding the Second Coming of Jesus Christ), and
that the events to bring on Armageddon, the end of the
world, would have their origin in a confrontation with the
United States government. He fully anticipated an armed
confrontation with the federal government would bring

the prophecies of the Book of Revelation, the last book of the Bible, to fruition. In preparation for the battle, Koresh and his followers held regularly scheduled target practice with AR-15 rifles and handguns. Koresh likened an altercation with the government to the Biblical battles against Babylon and Assyria.

Upon learning of the approaching ATF agents this Sunday morning, Koresh had the older women and children lay on the floor of the second floor hallway, away from the outer walls of the compound. The men and some of the women armed themselves with 9-mm pistols, automatic and semiautomatic assault rifles, and dressed in bulletproof vests and ammunition vests.

The sequence of events that followed remain unclear. Siege survivors relate that at approximately 9:45 A.M., two cattle trailers pulled by pickup trucks sped on to the Mount Carmel property. ATF agents began running towards the building. Intending to negotiate, an unarmed Koresh opened the left side of the double-sided front doors and stepped outside. "Police! Search warrant! Get down!" the agents ordered him. Ignoring their command, he yelled to them there were woman and children in the building. When the agents continued to press forward, Koresh quickly backed into the building and slammed the door. A barrage of bullets hit the door, striking Perry Jones, Koresh's father-in-law and chief assistant.

"They just started firing. I fell back in the door, and the bullets started coming through. I yelled, 'Go away, there's women and children here, let's talk,'" survivor David Thibodeau recalls Koresh explaining. By law, the agents had to announce the search warrant. Koresh was later to say he did not understand what the ATF agents were yelling as they ran towards him.

According to a September 1993 report issued by the

Department of the Treasury, gunfire first burst through the front door from the inside out, and then from every window in the front of the compound. A year later at a trial held in San Antonio of surviving Branch Davidians accused of murder, conspiracy, and firearms charges, three journalists and more than 20 ATF agents participating in the ground assault corroborated these findings, and testified the first shots fired on February 28 came from inside the compound.

Three other individuals, however, two of whom were ATF agents, testified the ATF fired first, but not on the residents of Mount Carmel. Several ATF agents had been assigned to the "dog team." Their assignment was to neutralize the five Alaskan malamute dogs, pets of the Mount Carmel children, kept in a fenced in area near the compound. One possible explanation for the discrepancy of who shot first is that members of the dog team fired the first shots at the dogs, and the residents, fearing they were being fired upon, fired back in self-defense.

For almost two hours, gunfire came from both sides. It is estimated that 10,000 rounds of ammunition were expended in the raid.

ATF agents assumed Koresh would be hiding in the gun room on the second floor over the chapel. Using 20-foot aluminum ladders to climb onto the roof, the agents attempted to gain access to the second floor from both the north and south sides of the building. The plan was to invade Koresh's bedroom and the gun room, secure the two second story rooms, and neutralize and arrest the occupants. Then the agents were to proceed to the gymnasium, where they would rendezvous with other agents who had entered the building via the first floor.

Smashing the windows in a "break and rake" procedure, ATF agents threw "flashbangs" (distraction grenades that produce a loud noise and a flash of bright light) into the room. From inside, Branch Davidians fired on the agents, killing two agents and injuring two. One agent, although shot six times, was able to crawl to the edge of the roof and fall to the courtyard below. Two other agents were killed outside the building.

While gunfire exploded from every direction, three National Guard helicopters, a UH-60 Blackhawk and two OH-58 Jet Rangers, carrying armed ATF troops dressed in riot gear hung over the compound. They fired down into the part of the building that housed the residential tower and chapel. Two helicopters were hit by gunfire and had to land nearby, while the third continued firing into the building. Autopsies later performed on the Mount Carmel residents killed in the raid showed some of the deaths came from bullets fired above them, presumably from the helicopters.

Five reporters of the *Waco Tribune-Herald* observed the raid from the property of a house across the street from the compound and were forced into a ditch by flying bullets. Photographers from KWTX-TV filmed the raid from the compound's driveway.

At 9:48 A.M., three minutes after the gunfire started, Wayne Martin, a Branch Davidian resident and a lawyer with an office inside Mount Carmel Center, dialed 911. "Call it off! There are women and children in here!" he is heard yelling on the audiotape recording of the call. "We want a cease-fire! If they don't back off, we're going to fight to the last man." Deputy Lieutenant Larry Lynch took the call. Because he had no authority to grant a cease-fire, he attempted to contact the ATF agents at Mount Carmel using a prearranged plan to announce himself on the sheriff's radio band, which was to be monitored by ATF. None

of the raiders on the ground had a cell phone, so direct communication was not possible. Instead, messages were routed to the ATF command center at Texas State Technical College via a campus policeman with a radio, who then got word to the ATF command post to contact Lynch. By 10:25 A.M., Lieutenant Lynch was in contact with the ATF command team, negotiating a cease-fire. Eventually two channels of communication were used to negotiate the cease-fire. ATF Special Agent James Cavanaugh, located in Rodriqez's undercover house, negotiated by phone with Koresh, while Lynch was on another phone line with Steve Schneider,

Black Hawk UH-60 helicopters like these fired into the residential tower and chapel at the Mount Carmel Center.

one of Koresh's right hand men, and Martin. By noon, a cease-fire was in effect.

In addition to the four dead ATF agents, there were 16 injured. Not expecting casualties of this magnitude, ATF had not made arrangements for adequate ambulance coverage, and their wounded were transported to Hillcrest Baptist Medical Center in a TV station van. One ATF agent with a chest wound was lying across the hood of the van, while others balanced on the side of the van, clinging to partially rolled down windows.

Five Branch Davidians were killed and four were wounded. Autopsies performed later showed two of the four had been shot at close range, apparent suicides or mercy killings by other Branch Davidians after the assault ended. Later that evening, snipers in the woods surrounding Mount Camel killed a sixth Branch Davidian as he attempted to return to the compound.

ATF agents claimed they had been ambushed and outgunned by the Branch Davidians. The Branch Davidians said they were attacked first and fought in self-defense. They referred to their call to 911 to illustrate their non-confrontional position.

Martin refused medical help for the Mount Carmel wounded, one of whom was David Koresh. Though seriously injured by one bullet that entered and exited his lower left torso, and another that injured his left hand, Koresh recovered and was able to give interviews to CNN and Dallas radio station KRLD the evening of the raid. Koresh attempted to explain his views of the raid in relation to apocalyptic events predicted in the Bible. When KRLD station manager asked him if he had any sympathy for the ATF agents killed and injured, Koresh replied, "My friend, it was unnecessary."

Several concerns precipitated the February 28 raid on the Branch Davidians by ATF. In 1989 several

Branch Davidians had left Mount Carmel over a disagreement in interpretation of doctrine. Now living in Australia, Marc Breault, Koresh's former right hand man, led the group. Breault hired a private investigator to gather information to corroborate the incidents of child abuse he had witnessed while living at Mount Carmel. Texas State and Federal agencies were contacted, yet neither found cause for the allegations. A second attempt a year later also failed. In early 1992 on Breault's urging, Australia's National Nine Network sent a team of reporters and photographers to Waco to produce a story on David Koresh and the Branch Davidians. The one-hour report broadcasted only on Australian television accused Koresh of punishing the sect's children by beating them, starving them, and depriving them of food and water.

Breault continued to press his allegations in Waco. Eventually his charges came to the attention of the Texas Department of Protection and Regulatory Services. Despite reports of child abuse by the former compound members, the assigned social worker could not verify the charges and closed the case on April 30, 1992.

Parallel to child abuse allegations, it was well known among the Branch Davidians that Koresh had taken several underage girls, some as young as eleven years old, as "wives." It was alleged that he had fathered at least 15 children by all his wives. According to Texas law, a woman must be 17 years old to have sexual relations. (This age, called the age of consent, varies from state to state.) In Texas, girls may marry at age 14 with parental permission. A sexual relationship with a girl under the age of consent and outside of marriage is called statutory rape, and in Texas, it is a first-degree felony, punishable by a prison sentence of 5 to 95 years. When a girl under the age of 17 gives birth, the baby's father can be charged with aggravated sexual assault. Many of Koresh's relationships made him guilty of both statutory rape and aggravated sexual assault.

The Texas Department of Protection and Regulatory Services was only one of several agencies interested in the Branch Davidians. In 1992 a UPS driver making a routine delivery to the "Mag Bag" auto shop noticed a partially opened package contained dummy grenades. He reported it to McLennan County Sheriff's Department who notified the Austin Bureau of Alcohol, Tobacco and Firearms. Special Agent Davy Aquilera of the Austin ATF office was assigned to investigate further the allegations that the Branch Davidians might be stockpiling weapons.

Former Branch Davidian members interviewed by Special Agent Aquilera told him Koresh maintained an armed guard at Mount Carmel 24 hours a day and that he possessed a loaded firearm at all times. It was also alleged that Koresh was preparing a "hit list" of former followers who were complaining to the authorities about his weapon stockpiling, among other things.

By checking UPS shipping and sales records, Aquilera learned that over a period of time, 90 pounds of powdered aluminum, as well as black gunpowder, had been delivered to Mount Carmel. When mixed together, the two substances are used in the manufacture of hand grenades, an activity prohibited by federal firearm laws. The two substances can also be used to reload spent rifle cartridges, which is not an illegal activity.

Other invoices showed that Koresh and other residents had purchased 104 "upper receivers" for AR-15 rifles. "Upper receivers" when matched with altered "lower receivers" can be used to convert legal semiautomatic

Branch Davidians Steve and Judy Schneider, shown here in a photo taken on their wedding day, died at the siege of Mt. Carmel.

AR-15s to illegal automatic M-16s. According to the National Firearms Act, automatic M-16s may be lawfully purchased or made in the United States after obtaining a clearance from local authorities and paying a $200 per weapon registration fee. Approval must be granted by the secretary of the treasury. No one at Mount Carmel, however, had applied for a permit to manufacture the M-16s.

The focus of Aquilera's investigation encompassed the illegal manufacture of machine guns from component parts, and the illegal manufacture and possession of destructive devices, including explosive bombs and grenades, and the materials necessary to make them. On July 30, 1992, Special Agents Davy Aquilera and Jimmy Skinner visited a local federally registered gun dealer, Henry McMahon, who operated a business called Hewlett Handguns. While checking Hewlett Handguns' invoices, they came across records indicating the purchase of 100 AR-15 lower receivers, which are classified as firearms. Many of the receivers weren't listed as being sold, yet they couldn't be accounted for in Hewlett Handguns' inventory.

McMahon explained to the agents that the gun parts were stored at Mount Carmel, where there was a safe large enough to hold them. Transfer of AR-15s must be registered in the National Firearms Registration and Transfer Record; however, McMahon could supply no record of the transfer.

Koresh realized that by purchasing the components of AR-15s, he could manufacture them at a price that would undercut gun show dealers. McMahon explained the partnership arrangement whereby Hewlett Handguns would purchase mail order lower receivers for Koresh, who would have the Branch Davidians manufacture A-15s. After assembled, Hewlett Handguns would sell the guns, splitting the profit between Hewitt Handguns and the Branch Davidians.

While Aquilera and Skinner were visiting McMahon on July 30, 1992, McMahon called Koresh, who invited the agents to Mount Carmel to see the inventory for themselves. "If there'a a problem, tell them to come out here. If they want to see my guns, they're more than welcome," Koresh told McMahon. The agents declined the invitation. This inquiry by ATF gave the Branch Davidians their first indication that they and their weapons were the focus of a federal investigation.

On January 11, 1993, ATF set up an "undercover house" in a vacant house across the driveway from Mount Carmel. The house was equipped with surveillance equipment. Special Agent Robert Rodriguez was one of eight men living in the home. On several occasions he visited the compound, attending Bible studies with the Branch Davidians and participating in target practice with them. Rodriquez and the other undercover agents were under orders by their superiors to determine whether there were armed guards at Mount Carmel, to identify counter surveillance, and to gather information relative to firearm violations.

Aquilera's investigation led him to check the backgrounds of all Mount Carmel residents. He learned that several had either been arrested, convicted, or were under investigation for crimes ranging from fraud, to smuggling and narcotics offenses. More than 40 residents were citizens of foreign countries living in the United States as illegal aliens. It is unlawful for either an illegal alien or a person convicted of a crime punishable by more than one year of imprisonment to possess any type of firearm.

Acting on a tip that the Koreshans might be involved in illegal manufacture of methamphetamines (drugs), Aquilera ordered a plane equipped with infrared sensors to fly over the compound searching for "hot spots" which would indicate production of the drugs.

Putting together the information he had acquired from former Branch Davidians and gun suppliers, Aquilera wrote an affidavit of probable cause and applied for a warrant to search Mount Carmel Center and the "Mag Bag." Although ATF had no jurisdiction over the making of drugs, the polygamy, child abuse, and statutory rape charges, these allegations were also included in the affidavit. United States Magistrate Dennis Green, a judge for the United States District Court for the western district of Texas, signed the search warrant on February 25, 1993, three days before the siege.

The poorly written affidavit contained many false and misleading statements. Koresh's invitation to Special Agent Aquilera to visit Mount Carmel to view the weapons was omitted. The residents of Mount Carmel possessed appropriate amounts of legally purchased ammunition, and the affidavit listed Koresh's possession of legal weapons as a reason to search the compound. The affidavit did not show intent on Koresh's part to sell the firearms, as required by law.

Still, federal authorities needed to see what was going on at Mount Carmel Center. By the end of 1992 the Branch Davidians knew the United States government was watching them very closely.

On the afternoon of February 28 raid, the FBI sent members of its Hostage Rescue Team (HRT) and Special Weapons and Tactics (SWAT) Team to Mount Carmel. Monday, March 1, the day after the raid, at the request of ATF, the Federal Bureau of Investigation (FBI) assumed control. Negotiations for conditions of surrender continued around the clock. Federal agents offered Koresh the opportunity to make a tape for broadcast by a national radio network; in return all residents of Mount Carmel would vacate the compound. By dawn on Tuesday, March 2, buses secured by the FBI were waiting to transport the Branch Davidians off the premises. Koresh's taped 58-minute message had aired several times on the Waco affiliate of the

David Koresh, in a 1981 photo taken at the Mount Carmel Center, was brought up in the Seventh Day Adventist Church.

Christian Broadcast Network. All seemed to be going according to schedule when Koresh sent Schneider to relay a message to the rest of the Branch Davidians. The group would not be surrendering after all. "We're not going. The time's not right," said Schneider. God had told Koresh to wait. Thus began the 51-day siege at Waco.

THE ATF AND THE FBI

The ATF consists of 4,000 personnel. In 1862 an act of Congress created an Office of Internal Revenue within the Treasury Department, assigning it the responsibility of collecting taxes on distilled spirits and tobacco products. Congress also authorized the hiring of three officers to enforce tax collection and deal with evaders. During Prohibition (the early part of the 20th century, when it was illegal to make, consume, or purchase alcohol), the officers were called "revenuers" and were responsible for enforcing the Prohibition laws, bringing, for the first time, tax collection and enforcement under one roof. In 1927 the Treasury Department elevated the Prohibition Unit to Bureau status. When the 21st Amendment to the Constitution repealed Prohibition, President Franklin Roosevelt established the Federal Alcohol Control Administration (FACA). A year later FACA was abolished by the Federal Alcohol Administration Act. The FAA functioned independently within the Department of the Treasury and in 1940 merged with the Alcohol Tax Unit, which was under the Bureau of Internal Revenue, Department of the Treasury.

The widespread use of weapons during Prohibition led to the passage of the National Firearms Act in 1934, followed four years later by the Federal Firearms Act. Enforcement and collection of fees fell to the Alcohol Tax Unit. In 1952 the Alcohol Tax Unit was renamed the Alcohol and Tobacco Tax Division. When the Gun Control Act was passed in 1968, the agency was renamed yet another time to the Alcohol, Tobacco and Firearms (ATF) Division. ATF is headquartered in Washington, D.C., although many operations are conducted throughout the country. ATF agents are involved in investigating some of the most violent crimes in society and in regulating some of the most important and sensitive industries in America. The agency enforces the federal laws and regulations relating to alcohol, tobacco, firearms and explosives, and arson.

The Federal Bureau of Investigation also has evolved via a circuitous route over the years. It originated in 1908 during President Theodore Roosevelt's presidency. At the time, the establishment of a federal investigative service was highly controversial. Prior to the formation of the FBI, the Department of Justice called upon the Secret Service to conduct investigations. On July 26, 1908, 10 former Secret Service officially became employees of the Department of Justice, forming a Bureau of Investigation. This represented the beginnings of the modern day FBI.

The Bureau of Investigation investigated federal crimes that involved national banking, bankruptcy, naturalization, and land fraud. No training was given for the

J. Edgar Hoover (1895-1972) was director of the U.S. Federal Bureau of Investigation (FBI) from 1924 until his death in 1972.

position, so previous law enforcement experience was desirable.

By 1917 when the United States entered World War I, there were more than 300 Special Agents and an additional 300 support employees. The Bureau of Investigation was headquartered in Washington and had field offices located in major cities of several states. A Special Agent in Charge, who reported to Washington, supervised each field office. By 1924 the Bureau had doubled again to over 600 employees.

Under J. Edgar Hoover's term as director of the Bureau in the 1920s, a formal training program was begun. Hoover also required agents to be between the ages of 25 and 35. Tracking criminals by means of identification records, including fingerprints began in the 1920s. In 1932 an early precursor to the FBI's "10 Most Wanted List" first became available. It was called "Fugitives Wanted by Police."

The Bureau of Investigation was re-named the United States Bureau of Investigation on July 1, 1932, and in 1935 its name was changed again to the Federal Bureau of Investigation.

In the 1990s the FBI began using DNA technology to positively identify or rule out suspects by comparing their DNA patterns. A national DNA index, similar to the fingerprint index of the 1920s, was created.

Modern day involvement of the FBI has included the Siege at Waco, the Bombing of the World Trade Center in 1993, and the Oklahoma City Bombing.

The Sinful Messiah

William Miller predicted the Second Coming of Christ would occur on October 23, 1844. The 1848 William Miller Chapel is located in Hampton, New York.

2

T he word "advent" means arrival. To Christians, the season of Advent is four weeks in the liturgical calendar immediately prior to Christmas, when they await the arrival or birth of the Messiah, Jesus Christ. Members of the Seventh Day Adventist Church base their faith in God as revealed through Jesus Christ and as shown through the Bible, inspired by the Holy Spirit. Their name reflects the religion's conviction of the nearness of the soon advent (return) of Jesus Christ, as promised and prophesied. However, modern day Adventists predict no date for the event. Seventh Day refers to the Biblical Sabbath, the seventh day of the week or Saturday, which modern day Adventists observe as the Sabbath Day. Currently there are 8 million Seventh Day Adventists worldwide; 750,000 are living in the United States.

Adventists abstain from caffeine, drugs, alcohol and tobacco, and believe in gun control.

The Adventist Church, also known as Adventism, was born on October 23, 1844, the day referred to as the Great Disappointment. Traditionally, the Seventh Day Adventist religion has had a history of separatism from other faiths, claiming to be the exclusive truth. In the last 50 years, Adventism has been welcomed by mainstream evangelical Christian faiths, losing much of their sectarian status.

According to Baptist farmer William Miller, during the calamitous times directly before the Apocalypse, only the most devout of Christians would be separated from the rest of mankind and allowed to be a part of the Second Coming of Christ. Miller predicted the Second Coming would occur on October 23, 1844. He based his insight on his interpretation of Daniel 8:14 found in the Old Testament. When the expected Second Coming did not occur, Miller maintained his faith in God and the Bible, and continued to preach the return of Jesus was imminent.

Miller's protégé, Ellen Gould Harmon White, or Sister White, as she was called, was a visionary who espoused keeping Saturday (the Seventh Day) holy as the Sabbath day. She argued that Miller had the correct date for the Second Coming of Christ, but he had been wrong about the event. According to Sister White, October 23 was the date Christ entered the inner room of the Heavenly Temple in preparation for judgment day. In addition to doctrine, Sister White preached the benefits of a pure diet. One of her most significant teachings dealt with the Adventists' relationship to the government. Sister White instilled in her followers a distrust of the government and urged them to keep themselves apart from governmental affairs.

In 1863 Sister White's followers were organized into the General Conference of Seventh Day Adventists (SDA). Quoting Revelation 14, she referred to herself as "the Third Angel." When she died in 1915 at the age of 88, she left an admonition that only those to whom God appears in dreams and visions are able to teach the scriptures, and that more visionaries would appear after her death.

In the late 1920s Victor Houteff, an immigrant from Bulgaria and a follower of Sister White, fell out of favor with mainstream Adventists when he began publishing criticisms of California SDA leaders. In 1934 Houteff and about a dozen families founded a community of Adventists 10 miles outside of Waco, Texas. In the Old Testament Book of Elijah, the prophet went to war with the followers of the pagan god Baal at a place called Mount Carmel. It was after this biblical Mount Carmel that Houteff named the site where his followers would live and pray.

Distancing his group from the Seventh Day Adventists, Houteff called his community "The Shepherd's Rod." Later they became known as the Davidian Seventh Day Adventist Association. He believed himself to be a present day Elijah who would prepare King David's throne for the advent of the Messiah, expected by the Jews, or the Second Coming of Christ, as Christians viewed the event. At this time, Houteff would bring all his followers to Jerusalem to welcome the advent.

Houteff's Mount Carmel was constructed in such a way as to test the ability of his followers to withstand the "withering experience"—a means of denying the pleasures of the flesh in order to conquer the spirit, thereby proving oneself to be a follower of God and not of Baal. The group adhered to an Adventist diet: no

Victor Houteff, founder of the Mount Carmel Adventists, believed he was a present day Elijah, who would prepare King David's throne for the Second Coming of Christ.

sugar and milk mixtures, caffeine, white flour, pork, or other foods banned by an Orthodox Jewish diet as being unclean. Living conditions were primitive.

In the 1950s Houteff began having health problems, and after his death a rivalry for his successor arose. Florence Houteff, his widow, believed that before his death, Houteff had revealed to her the date of "End Time" to be April 22, 1959. Ben Roden, leader of another Seventh Day Adventist splinter group called "The Branch," and his wife, Lois, challenged Florence for Houteff's position as leader of the community. When

"End Time" did not occur on April 22, 1959, members Houteff's sect switched their loyalty to the Roden's.

Ben Roden died in 1978 and Lois became his successor. Once again the name of the religious group was changed, this time to the "Living Waters Branch." In 1977 Lois had declared the Holy Spirit to be feminine, a teaching the Seventh Day Adventist clergy condemned as heresy. Her theories caused her to be expelled from the Seventh Day Adventist General Conference in Dallas. The year was 1980. The same year Lois Roden was ousted by her religion, 21-year-old Vernon Howell entered her life.

The man the world has come to know as David Koresh was born Vernon Wayne Howell in Houston, Texas, on August 17, 1959. His mother, Bonnie Clark, was only 14 years old, and his parents were not married. Shortly after Howell was born, Bonnie married another man. This marriage was short-lived, as Bonnie's new husband physically abused his stepson.

By the time Howell was five, Bonnie was married to Roy Haldeman and living in Dallas. Roy called Howell "Sputnik" because of his hyperactivity. Bonnie and Roy started their own construction cleanup business. Howell spent time fishing with his grandfather on the weekends, and he learned to hunt. Both of Howell's parents beat him as a child, and his cousins tried to sexually molest him.

Howell suffered from dyslexia, a learning disability that causes the eye to read the letters of a word in an inverted order. As a result of his disability, Howell did poorly in school, failing the first grade twice and the second grade once. He also stuttered. His mother sent him to a special school where the class size was smaller and extra attention from the teacher more available. Schoolmates and friends made fun of him, calling him "Mr. Retardo."

In high school he was an average student who dropped out in 11th grade. His hobbies were playing the guitar, and tinkering with car motors and other machinery. "I could understand machines, like cars, engines, radios, anything I could put my hands on and take apart to see how they worked," he told one of his followers, David Thibodeau. "But reading and writing was a foreign language," Howell said, admitting that even as an adult he had trouble reading and writing.

Howell was brought up in the Seventh Day Adventist Church. Religion had an effect on him. He followed the evangelists whose message came through the TV and radio. By the time he was 12, Howell had memorized long passages of biblical scripture. In high school he conducted Bible studies for his fellow students. When he was 17, he was formally baptized into the Seventh Day Adventist Church.

"One time I played hooky from school and went to the church to talk to the Man Himself. On my knees, I prayed: 'Dear Father, I know I'm stupid, but please talk to me 'cause I want to serve you.' A while later I heard His word in my heart, as if we were discussing things directly," he told Thibodeau.

In 1977 at the age of 18, Howell fell in love with 16-year-old Linda Campion. Against the teachings of the Seventh Day Adventist Church, the two had sex. When confronted with her pregnancy, Howell denied he could be the father of her child, stating he was sterile. Howell broke off the relationship, and without his knowledge, Linda had an abortion.

Either a sense of religious guilt or obligation caused Howell to resume his love affair with her. " . . . That holy voice in my heart reminded me that, according to Scripture, since I'd been with her, had entered her body with mine, we were married in His eyes." A

few months later she was pregnant again. When he confessed to being the father of both babies, Linda's father forbade Howell from seeing her.

A few weeks afterward Howell had a religious experience where he claimed to have heard the voice of God. Howell said about his experience " . . . a voice imparted a picture completely perfect in my mind . . . and He says, 'You're really hurt, aren't you? You've loved her for about a year, and now she's turned her back on you . . . Don't you know that for 19 years I've loved you, and for 19 years

In the Seventh Day Adventist Church, the seventh day (Saturday) is observed as the Sabbath. Seventh Day Adventists look forward to the return of Jesus Christ as prophesied in the Bible.

you've turned your back on me and rejected me?'"

In what Howell calls a "marvelous moment of self-affirmation," he realized the one true purpose of his life was to be true to God's word. In this visionary experience, Howell thought he understood God to say he would give Linda back to him. "But He never did. I lost contact with her and our child, my firstborn."

Howell claimed his relationship with Linda brought him to God. "I couldn't make sense of the failure of our connection. It wrenched my gut. I had to find my way back to my true fate. It was waiting for me, I knew, out there somewhere," he told David Thibodeau.

One night in the late 1970s, Howell had a vision of God the Father holding out his hand to him. God's other hand held a book. The word "prophecy" was inscribed upon a wall. It was after this experience that he traveled to Mount Carmel. Lois Roden was in her sixties and her son, George, was planning to take over the sect when his mother died. Lois clearly favored Howell to be her successor over her son. When rivalry between the two men caused Howell to leave Mount Carmel, he settled in Palestine, Texas, in rural Anderson County, about 100 miles east of Mount Carmel. There Howell and a small group of followers lived in flimsy lean-tos, shacks, and tents.

Before leaving Mount Carmel, Howell married 14-year-old Rachel Jones, the daughter of Perry Jones, an elder in the Living Branch sect. Rachel and Koresh were to have two children, a son, Cyrus and a daughter, Star.

In 1985 while on a trip to Jerusalem, Howell experienced another vision. He claimed beings of light brought him face to face with God. He claimed God revealed to him the true "End Time" was to occur in 1995. According to Howell, God gave him the power to explain the Seven Seals of the Book of Revelation—the last book of the Bible which describes the end of the world.

The Fifth Book of Revelation reads:

And I saw a scroll in the right hand of the one who was sitting in the throne. There was writing on the inside and the outside of the scroll, and it was sealed with seven seals. And I saw a strong angel, who shouted with a loud voice: who is worthy to break the seals on this scroll and unroll it? But no one under the earth was able to open the scroll and read it.

Revelation goes on to proclaim that only the Lamb of God, the heir to the throne of David, is worthy to break the Seven Seals and read the scroll. Koresh claimed to be the Lamb of God. He saw the interpretation of the Seven Seals as being the starting point for the understanding of the rest of the Bible. According to Koresh, the Book of Revelation is the Truth of God, the Son. As Jesus had revealed the Truth of God the Father by his life, death, and resurrection, another Messiah would reveal the Truth of God, the Son. Unlike Jesus Christ, who was divine, the second messiah will have all of the traits of a man, including the ability to sin. Koresh believed he was the "Sinful Messiah."

The first four seals of the scroll unleash conquest, famine, war, and death. The fifth seal reveals the "souls of those who had been slain for the word of God." It reads:

And when the Lamb broke the fifth seal, I saw under the altar the souls of all who had been martyred for the word of God and for being faithful to their witness. They called loudly to the Lord and said, "O Sovereign Lord, holy and true, how long will it be for you judge the people who belong to this world for what they have done to us? When will you avenge our blood against these people? . . . Then they were told to rest a little longer until the full number of the servants of Jesus had been martyred.

Koresh's visions showed him that the person who

The Four Horsemen of the Apocalypse, War, Strife, Famine and Death, are described in the Book of Revelation, the last book in the New Testament. John the Apostle is thought to have written it, although other scholars believe it may have been written to comfort persecuted Christians during the Roman Empire.

opened or uncovered the Seven Seals would not only be able to explain the book, but would cause the events recorded in Revelation to come to pass. Koresh interpreted the fifth seal to be the February 28 assault. He often remarked, "We are in the fifth seal." The words "*rest a little longer*" was interpreted to mean the siege at Mount Carmel—the time the Branch Davidians were currently living through. Once the fifth seal had been opened, the breaking of the sixth seal would produce an earthquake, and the seventh seal would reveal seven angels who blow successively on trumpets, signaling the end of the world. After earthquakes, famines and plagues were unleashed, Jesus would return, and together with his followers, the final battle against evil would be fought.

Revelation speaks of the 24 elders from whom would descend the 144,000 true believers who will surround the Lamb of God when he appears at End Time. The 144,000 would be spared the Apocalypse. Koresh believed his children to be the 24 elders. In the coming Kingdom of God, these children would be rulers with the Lamb.

Many opinions exist about the Book of Revelation. The author's name is simply John. He is believed to have been a Jew-turned-Christian who wrote 70 years after the birth of Christ. Some feel the book has more to do with the dealings of the Roman Empire at the end of the first century than it does with the spirituality of mankind. Some religions view Revelation as being the written record of visions experienced by the author. Other faiths interpret the Book of Revelation literally and see it as a true prophecy of the last days of the world.

Koresh returned from Israel a newly energized for ministry. He believed his body and soul had been re-created into a whole new person. According to Koresh, he never had to study the Bible after his revelation in Israel. Meanings would simply "fall into place." A voice gave him new insights. He visualized the Bible in his mind. He became "the Seventh Angel."

Koresh believed he was the final prophet of the world, whose mission it was to save as many people as he could before the Apocalypse brought a bloody confrontation with the authorities that was necessary to bring an end to the world. Furthermore, those he saved would reign with Christ on His right hand side in the Kingdom of God.

After a 1987 shoot-out, former leader George Roden lost control of the Branch Davidians to David Koresh.

Lois Roden died in 1986, and after a shoot-out with George in which Howell gained control of the Branch Davidians, he and a small group moved back to Mount Carmel. In 1990 Howell legally changed his name to David Koresh. He told the court he was an entertainer, and he needed the new name for publicity. Religious significance, however, lies beneath the new first and last name. In the Old Testament Book of the Prophet Isaiah, the ancient King Cyrus who triumphed over the Babylonians in 539 B.C. freed the Jews and helped them rebuild their destroyed temple. Isaiah referred to Cyrus as a messiah, the Hebrew word for "anointed one." In Hebrew, the word "Cyrus" is Koresh.

Howell's confrontation with George Roden gave the government its first indication of the military potential of the Branch Davidians. For David Koresh who believed himself to be the reincarnation of King Cyrus, winning back Mount Carmel was part of God's plan. Also in God's plan was the battle of Armageddon between good and evil that the Book of Revelation revealed would occur at the end of time. According to the Branch Davidians, the ATF raid had fulfilled Koresh's prophecies. His modern day Babylon was the government of the United States of America.

Mount Carmel—Cult or Congregation?

The forces of Cyrus II began a conquest of Babylon in 539 B.C. The Prophet Isaiah referred to Cyrus as a messiah. The word "Cyrus" is Koresh in Hebrew.

3

The Branch Davidians of Mount Carmel were a Christian community who called God the Father by his Hebrew name, "Yeshua." Their Sabbath was observed on Saturday as a day of prayer; no outside work or discussions were allowed on the Sabbath. They observed all of the Jewish Holidays, but did not observed Christmas or Easter.

The group became known as the "Branch Davidians" because the deed to Mount Carmel was in the name of Ben Roden's sect, the Branch Davidians Seventh Day Adventist Association. "None of us here have ever called ourselves twigs or branches or roots or anything else," Steve Schneider explained, stating that Koresh's followers preferred to call themselves students of the Seven Seals or Koreshans.

The community living at Mount Carmel on February 28 was multi-ethnic and multi-racial. Koresh had recruited members from Britain, the United States, Canada, Mexico, Israel, the Philippines, New Zealand, Australia, and the Caribbean Islands. Several people were of African American, Asian, and European decent. Many had let their visas expire for fear of being sent back to their countries. They were a cross section of economically rich and poor. Some of the residents were highly educated; Steve Schneider had a degree in theology, and Wayne Martin was a lawyer. Others had little or no education. While some of the residents had lived at Mount Carmel with the Rodens in the 1950s, Koresh had recruited most in the 1980s and 1990s. All of his followers took Koresh as their last name. With a few exceptions, all the Branch Davidians came from a Seventh Day Adventist background.

Koresh often used music to recruit new followers. He handed out business cards for "Messiah Productions." The cards read "David Koresh, Musician" and "Steve Schneider, Agent."

The Mount Carmel Compound was located on a dirt road called Double E Ranch Road. The main building at Mount Carmel was a city block long. It was beige in color, an "L" shaped wooden structure, assembled from the recycled materials of the shacks and cottages that had sheltered the Branch Davidians upon their return to Mount Carmel from Palestine, Texas. Inside, the residents ate, slept, worked, and prayed. As Koresh's message grew increasingly more apocalyptic, the residents began referring to Mount Carmel as "Ranch Apocalypse." Others refered to it as the "Camp" or the "Anthill," the later because of the fire ants that seemed to be everywhere. A Star of David flag flew from a flag post in front of the compound.

Mount Carmel's lower floor housed a kitchen, cafeteria, pantry area for food storage, and a concrete walk-in cooler. The cooler was a room fortified with one-foot thick concrete walls on all sides. It was used for food and record storage. The cooler formed the base for three stories of bedrooms, referred to by the residents as the residential tower. In the government reports after the siege and fire, the cooler was referred to as a "bunker."

Also downstairs were a telephone room and a computer room. A chapel with a stage and a gymnasium, used for storage at the time of the siege, formed the base of the "L." Upstairs, above the chapel stage were Koresh's bedroom, a gun room, and a hallway. A series of underground tunnels and a buried school bus served as a tornado shelter. An in-the-ground swimmimg pool was under construction.

The only running water at Mount Carmel was in the kitchen. There were no bathroom facilities; men used an outhouse, and women and children used chamber pots, and emptied them in a specially designated location away from the house. Men showered outside; women and children bathed from basins inside.

Except for Koresh's bedroom, Mount Carmel had no central heating or air-conditioning. During the winter, space heaters generated warmth in the spartan, unpainted rooms. There was a reason for the primitive nature of the buildings, Koresh explained to newcomers. He wanted to be sure people were coming to Mount Carmel to hear the Biblical message and not for the accommodations. It was a modern day rendition of Houteff's "withering experience."

The meals served at Mount Carmel followed a rationed vegetarian diet. Breakfast was cereal and fruit. Lunch might be a small salad, and dinner often was popcorn and peanuts. The members of the commune were frequently required to fast.

Koresh's diet, however, included meat and beer. He had a TV in his room, and while his followers rose before dawn, Koresh often stayed in bed until early afternoon, watching MTV.

The day's activities revolved the around prayer. Twice a day according to Old Testament traditions, on the third and ninth hour from sunrise, a religious service followed by communion was held in the chapel. Bible study often followed. The women cooked, did chores, and helped one another take care of the children. They sewed "Koresh Survival Wear"—hunting garments that were sold by the men at the gun shows. The women wore modest clothes and no makeup, and wore their hair long. The men worked around the compound, or in the auto shop, or landscaping business. The children were home schooled and were rarely allowed off the grounds of the compound. They were not allowed to watch TV, eat candy, or drink soda. All of the children, Koresh's as well as the others, were disciplined by beatings with a wooden paddle.

The cost of living at Mount Carmel was $15,000 a month, approximately $125 per person. Several members worked outside the compound as nurses and mechanics, and donated their paychecks back to the sect. Others gave Koresh their social security checks, pensions, and other governmental subsidies. Many members gave everything they owned to Koresh when they joined the Branch Davidians. One elderly couple gave Koresh a half a million dollars. One family donated a house, as well as a van.

According to Branch Davidian Paul Fatta who wasn't at the compound the day of the raid, firearms were kept to defend the group against attack by former Branch

Davidians. A select group of followers whom Koresh called his "Mighty Men" were allowed to possess weapons and guarded Mount Carmel. The term "Mighty Men" comes from the Biblical men who guard King Solomon's bed. Yet despite the propensity for violence, Koresh's neighbors thought the Branch Davidians were polite and well behaved, and saw them more as clannish members of a religious community then a dangerous cult.

Anyone who wished to come to Mount Carmel to hear Koresh teach the Bible was welcome to visit and stay at Mount Carmel as long as he wished. The group celebrated the Jewish holidays of Passover in the spring and the Festival of Tabernacles in the fall. During both feasts, Mount Carmel would be packed with individuals

David Koresh is pictured here in happier times with his mother, his wife Rachel, and his two children Star and Cyrus. Rachel and the two children were among the 82 victims of the siege at Waco.

and families. A mesmerizing speaker, Koresh would teach his interpretations of the Bible to his followers for hours, often far into the night. In addition to Koresh, Schneider, and another resident, Sherri Jewell, taught doctrine. All who wished to continue their studies at Mount Carmel were invited to move in permanently.

In 1989 Koresh received his "New Light" revelation, and married couples living at Mount Carmel were no longer allowed to sleep together. Koresh annulled (declared invalid) their marriages. All men, whether married or single, slept in dormitory-type rooms off a long first floor hallway. Women with children slept in identical rooms upstairs, and women with no children slept in a separate room off the second floor hallway. The men and women ate separately, and there was little communication between "once married" couples.

Koresh required his male followers to follow a celibate (the absence of sexual activity) lifestyle. According to the "New Light" revelation, women were allowed to have sexual relations only with Koresh. As the Lamb of God, Koresh believed he could have a sexual relationship with any of the women and girls at Mount Carmel, all of whom he considered to be his "spiritual wives." Girls as young as 10 years old knew they had been chosen to be a wife when they were given a gold Star of David necklace to wear. The women and girls he had a sexual relationship with were called his "carnal wives." Koresh had fathered approximately 15 children by all his carnal wives. He believed his offspring would become the 24 elders from whom the 144,000 to be carried to heaven would be born. He wanted the woman who would bear his children to have a purity in body and spirit that he could hold up to the rest of the world. Koresh was trying to create an army from his seed, and according to him, he was providing God with grandchildren. For the women to resist this

David Koresh identified with the Star of David symbol, reflecting the connection he felt to King David. The Star of David flag flew in front of the Mount Carmel Center.

thinking would be to go against God's will. Koresh's polygamy was a biblical trial for the men of the sect.

His pupils believed that Koresh's teachings were the guarantee of eternal salvation. To be "in the message" was to be a faithful follower of what God was currently revealing to the prophets, specifically, Koresh, who believed God had given him the assignment to carry out the major events which would lead to the end of the world. To prepare his followers for battle, Koresh had them repeatedly watch war movies such as *Hamburger Hill, Full Metal Jacket,* and *Platoon.* Both men and women were required to keep themselves in shape by lifting weights, performing military-type drills, and running obstacle courses.

By 1989 a combination of Koresh's teachings and sexual behavior convinced Branch Davidian, Marc Breault, that Koresh was a false prophet. In their book *Inside the Cult,* Breault and co-author Martin King of Australia's National Nine News's show, *A Current Affair,* exposed all the negative connotations associated with cults that took place at Mount Carmel. Included are allegations of abuse of children and adults, violence, and Koresh's domination of his followers. King stated that by featuring Koresh on his show, he wished to expose Koresh as a "cruel, maniacal, child-molesting, pistol-packing religious zealot who brainwashed his devotees into having them believe he was the Messiah, the reincarnation of Jesus Christ, who would eventually lead them into an all-out war with the United States government, and finally to their deaths." Yet, despite the allegations in the book, Breault admits that followers submitted their judgment and decision making power willingly to Koresh. From the time they took notice of Koresh and the Branch Davidians, the media's allegations of sexual impropriety, child abuse, polygamy, and weapon stockpiling served to label the group at Mount Carmel a "dangerous cult."

The word "cult" comes from the Latin word *cultus*, a derivative of the word *colere*, which means "to worship." A cult is a group of people that forms around a leader who claims he or she is above the ordinary individual. Almost always self-appointed, the cult leader claims to have a special assignment to accomplish in either life or death, or professes to have a special gift or knowledge that will be shared with only those who acknowledge the leader, and are willing to turn over all their decision-making capabilities to him or her. It is estimated there are between 3,000 and 5,000 cults in the United States and as many as two to five million people are involved in any given cult at one time or another.

A historical study of cults reveals they are not a new phenomenon. Cults tend to flourish during times of political or social upheaval. Upheaval causes confusion which makes individuals vulnerable to those who claim to have the answers to all the problems of the world. Cults thrived after the fall of the Roman Empire, during the French Revolution, at the time of the Industrial Revolution, and right after World War II.

In the past, cults attracted people who were living on the fringes of society—those with no ties to work or family who were searching for a place to belong and a reason to live. These people are easy targets for cult leaders who prey on the emotionally needy by offering an alternative lifestyle. In the 1960s and 1970s, teenagers and young people in their twenties who became disenchanted with the political and social climate joined cults in search of a perfect society. Today, cult leaders recruit more middle-of-the-road individuals. The majority of adolescents and adults who join cults come from middle-class backgrounds and are fairly well educated. Most cults have no age requirement for joining, and teenagers are just as likely to be recruited as senior citizens. Entire families are often recruited together. Research shows two-thirds of people who join cults come from normally functioning families and demonstrate age-appropriate behavior at the time they joined the cult.

Many modern day cult recruits may be people who are at a vulnerable point in their lives, experiencing personal loss or transition. To such people in need, a cult appears to be the solution to their problems, and they willingly turn over their money, possessions, as well as their lives, to the cult leader who promises to give them the answers they seek.

A cult is an authoritarian (rigid, controlling, and almost dictatorial) society. The leader defines the cult and all its members, and the cult becomes a reflection of its leader's personality. The desires of the leader dictate every aspect of daily life. Cult members give their leaders total control over their lives. Cults have regulations affecting dress, diet, sexual relationships, parent-child relationships, where members will live, work, and pray. In many cults, as a test of their devotion to the cult leader, husbands must live apart from their wives and children from their parents.

A person with a charming or appealing personality is said to be charismatic. Many, but not all, cult leaders possess this type of personality. Of greater importance to the formation of a cult is the leader's ability to control the lives of cult members. Cult leaders use "thought control" to change their followers' behavior. Cult leaders often have followers leave homes and families to become dependent upon the leader and fully embrace the cultic lifestyle. As a full-fledged member of a cult, the follower may continue to be exposed to intense psychological stress from the leader and intense social pressure from other cult members.

There is much concern over the treatment of children living in cults. Neglect, poor nutrition, little or no schooling, poor medical and dental care, emotional and psychological abuse, and harsh discipline are many of the concerns of researchers studying cults. In some cults, the lives of the children are dictated by the cult leader, and even parents are powerless to intervene on their behalf. Studies of children who have left cults show they are unfamiliar with the emotional give and take which is a

Jim Jones, the cult leader of the People's Temple, claimed to be God and that he cured illnesses. He threatened to kill anyone if they left the group.

part of family life, including the earning and losing of privileges, and a healthy respect of consequences for actions taken. Children living in cults know only that they must obey and to not do so causes punishment.

Because there is often such little contact with the outside world, those who have lived in a cult for a number of years become estranged from family and friends. The cult has been their entire life, and returning to mainstream society requires assistance as the former cult member makes the transition from dependence to independence. This is called "deprogramming" or "reprogramming."

Some cult members never get the opportunity to leave their cults. This is illustrated by the fate of one of the most well-known cults in recent times, the People's Temple led by Jim Jones. Originally located in San Francisco, Jones moved his followers to a camp in the jungle outside Georgetown, Guyana, a small country in South America. He named his camp "Jonestown." Professing to be God, he pretended to read minds, cure tumors, and raise people from the dead. More than 900 people, including 276 children, lived at Jonestown.

Jones required extreme proof of loyalty of his followers by having them sign blank legal documents or false confessions admitting they had molested their children or planned to overthrow the United States government. Jones threatened to kill anyone who left his community. In November 1978 at the request of family members who claimed their loved ones were being held at Jonestown against their will, Congressman Leo Ryan of California flew to Guyana to confront Jones. Twelve of Jones's followers chose to return to the United States with Ryan, but as they were boarding their plane, Jones ordered his assistants to kill the entire group, including the Congressman.

Jones had several times tested the loyalty of his followers by conducting "suicide drills." After consuming a beverage, Jones would inform them it was poisoned. Now, knowing he would be charged with the death of Congressman Ryan, Jones orchestrated a suicide drill with a Kool-Aid type drink laced with cyanide. 912 members of the People's Temple died at Jonestown, including Jim Jones himself, who either committed suicide or was shot by one of his followers.

The mass suicide at Jonestown enlightened people to the existence of cults and the threats they may pose to individuals, as well as society. However, not all cults are

self-destructive, dangerous, or restrictive. For some individuals, cults provide a place in society and a sense of security that they would not otherwise have. Many Americans are quick to label non-traditional religions cults, yet the early days of numerous established religions, including Christianity, share many of the characteristics of a cult. In America, the beliefs and practices of all religious groups are constitutionally protected. Whether a cult or a congregation, the Branch Davidians were exercising one of the basic tenants upon which our country was founded—the freedom of religion.

In the mass suicide at the People's Temple at Jonestown in Guyana, South America, 912 people died, including Jim Jones.

On April 9, 1993, a heli-
copter is seen hovering
over the Branch Davidian
Compound.

The Siege

K oresh was seriously wounded in the February 28 raid by a bullet
that hit him in the left hip. He complained of numbness throughout his body. His blood pressure dropped, and several times he
lost consciousness. He also suffered from intense headaches and muscle
spasms. His wound continued to bleed, and he was urinating blood. In
addition to the bullet wound in his hip, Koresh's left wrist had also been hit
by a bullet, severing the nerve in his thumb. Throughout the siege, Branch
Davidian Annetta Richards, a nurse from Jamaica, monitored Koresh's
health inside the compound.

Despite his injuries, with Steve Schneider's assistance, Koresh was able
to begin telephone discussions with federal agents soon after the raid's
cease-fire. The first bargaining chips in the negotiations were Mount

Carmel's children. Koresh promised to send out a pair of children each time a message he wrote was broadcasted over radio station KRLD. Four children exited the compound the evening of February 28.

The following day, March 1, the FBI sent agents experienced in negotiations and crisis management to Mount Carmel, at the request of the Deputy Director of ATF Dan Hartnett. Special Agent-in-Charge (SAC) Jeffrey Jamar from San Antonio was responsible for the overall resolution of the standoff. SAC Jamar's team consisted of two sets of personnel: negotiators and tactical, including the FBI's Hostage Rescue Team (HRT) and Special Weapons and Tactics (SWAT) Team. Entering the picture after an armed confrontation was, to the FBI, working backwards to some extent, as there was no occasion for them to obtain intelligence and other information beforehand, as is usually the case.

With the FBI fully in charge of the siege, ATF took over the responsibility of establishing the security of the compound's outer perimeter, providing security for hospitalized agents and assisting with negotiations.

The raid on the Branch Davidian Compound made international news within hours of the cease-fire. During the seven-week siege, thousands of spectators camped out at the FBI's perimeter to watch the FBI and ATF operations. Many carried homemade signs protesting against the original assault and subsequent siege, or distributed pamphlets, or bumper stickers.

President Bill Clinton asked to be kept informed of the standoff and told Acting General Stuart Gerson he understood it to be the policy of the FBI to negotiate until the situation was resolved. At Mount Carmel, barring threat of imminent bodily harm or death, the rules of engagement would avoid any exchange of gunfire with those in the compound.

The FBI's goal was to get everyone out of the compound without further injury or loss of life. The FBI negotiators offered national exposure for Koresh on Ted Koppel's television show *Nightline* in return for the surrender of all of Mount Carmel's residents. Koresh declined the offer, stating that the decision to surrender was a personal one that each follower should decide for himself. However, when national publicity was offered a second time, he accepted, and made an audiotape to be played nationally over the Christian Broadcast Network's show *America Talks,* as well as locally over radio station KRLD. On the tape, Koresh preached about the Bible, his interpretation of the verses relating to the Seven Seals and the Book of Revelation's predictions about the end of the world. Craig Smith, host of *America Talks,* agreed to air the audiotape on the condition that Koresh surrender immediately after it was aired, and that Koresh specify on the tape that it was his intention to do so.

As part of the deal, the FBI insisted an adult resident bring the audiotape out of Mount Carmel. On March 2 two of the older residents, Margaret Lawson and Catherine Matteson, both in their seventies, delivered the 58-minute audiotape to the FBI. Two children accompanied them.

Lawson and Matteson were immediately arrested, and charged with murder and attempted murder of federal agents. Both were held without bail. Koresh and Schneider, angered by the treatment of the women, felt they had been tricked. Afraid the murder and attempted murder charges would jeopardize the surrender of the other Koreshans, the status of the two women was downgraded to being held as material witnesses.

The exact number was not clear, but it was estimated there were 43 men, 43 women, and 20 children remaining in the compound. Law enforcement agents, expecting a mass departure, had arranged for a streamlined processing, including medical attention if needed, of a large group of people. The surrendered Branch Davidians would walk through a metal detector and on to a bus that would take them to a processing center at Texas State Technical College. There they would be dressed in prison uniforms, photographed, and taken to local jails. Some of the Branch Davidians would be charged with the murder of the federal agents, and some would be held as material witnesses.

Meanwhile, still inside the compound, Koresh was discussing the order of evacuation with negotiators over the phone. Koresh would be taken out by stretcher first, accompanied by the women and children, followed by men with their hands raised. "That will be good for TV," Koresh explained. Schneider was to remain in the building and send out one resident every minute or two. Koresh's audiotape was aired over the Christian Broadcast Network on March 2, at 1:30 P.M. Texas time. The Koreshans packed their bags in preparation of their leaving Mount Carmel. By mid-afternoon, however, Koresh had called off the surrender. He had received God's message to wait.

During the 51-day siege, Koresh and Schneider dealt with two dozen negotiators. SAC Byron Sage took over the position of chief negotiator. Over the course of the siege, the Koreshans argued with the negotiators about religion, the criminal justice system, the press, and conditions of surrender. Often Koresh and Schneider would interject religious doctrine into the discussions and attempt to convert the negotiators. The FBI held both telephone and face-to-face discussions with approximately 54 Branch Davidians during the conflict, and conversations between Mount Carmel residents and

representatives of the government amount to 18,000 pages of transcripts.

Koresh and Schneider wanted the FBI to promise to bring to justice the ATF agents responsible for the Mount Carmel killings. They also wanted to know what charges would be made against the surviving members after they surrendered. The FBI agents could not say, citing it was out of their department and in the hands of the United States Attorney's office.

Although Koresh consistently denied the possibility, the FBI was concerned the Branch Davidians would commit mass suicide. Former Branch Davidians and experts on suicide who were consulted by the FBI gave conflicting information about the group's philosophy on

Janet Reno was named the first female attorney general by President Bill Clinton at the White House on February 12, 1993.

suicide. Kathy Schroeder, a Branch Davidian who left the compound on March 12 and later turned state's witness, guaranteed the FBI that suicide would not occur. Schroeder told the FBI there were residents who wished to leave but could not because they were under Koresh's control. This was contradicted by Schneider who said the residents were free to leave at any time; it was only Koresh that had been told by God to wait.

Family and friends of the residents arriving at Waco contacted the negotiators to ask about loved ones inside the compound. Schneider relayed messages back and forth between Branch Davidians and their relatives. He allowed the FBI to play taped messages from them over the phone to compound residents, and they, in turn, passed messages to those outside through the negotiators.

Between February 28 and March 23, 14 adults and 35 children left Mount Carmel. None of the children were Koresh's biological children. Photographs and videos of the children who had been released were sent to parents still in the compound. The mothers were unhappy to see their children fed candy, soda, and other junk food. The mothers also felt their children, as seen in the video, were behaving poorly. By playing on the parents' emotions, the FBI hoped to hasten the departure of the parents.

After the February 28 raid, Mount Carmel was virtually cut off from the outside world. The compound's satellite dish mounted on the roof had been damaged by gunfire, restricting the TV to one channel with poor reception. Mail delivery to the compound was stopped. The radios worked until the FBI cut off the electricity permanently on March 12. The two telephone lines in the compound were restricted and could only be dialed out to the negotiators.

The compound was fortified with enough canned goods and military-style Meals Ready to Eat (MREs) to last one year. Milk was in short supply, however, and on several occasions was delivered to the compound by the FBI. Mount Carmel residents used candles, kerosene, propane, and Coleman lanterns for light and had one gasoline-powered generator. Water rationing began early in April. Rainwater was collected in buckets and pails. Bathing was limited and drinking water was restricted to two 8-ounce ladles a day per person.

The lack of press and the presence of the armored vehicles on Mount Carmel property were the two main concerns of people inside. Despite repeated requests by Branch Davidians for media coverage, federal agents restricted members of the press to "Satellite City," a press area located two miles from the compound. On March 9 residents hung a bed sheet out the tower window on which was painted: "God help us, we want the press." Throughout the 51-day siege, the Branch Davidians were never given the opportunity to speak to the press. The FBI repeatedly told the Koreshans they would have access to the press only when they came out of the compound.

Because of FBI concerns that Koreshans moving in and around the compound could trigger an accidental gunfight, a statement of safety was read to Koresh early on in the siege. The statement said: "Rules for your safety: No one will be allowed to exit the building with a weapon. We tell you this for your own protection—for if our agents perceive that their lives or the life of someone else is at risk, they will take appropriate action to ensure their own safety. No one will be allowed to aim a weapon from a window as this may also be perceived by our agents as a threat to their lives, or to the lives of others, and compel them to act accordingly. Any time you exit the building, and are approaching our agents, you must fully comply with any verbal instruction to avoid exposing yourself to potential risk."

Despite the warning, the residents moved freely outside the building, emptying waste receptacles, feeding chickens, and smoking. By the first week in April, however, the FBI was throwing "flash bang" grenades at anyone who exited the building.

Koresh was suspected of restricting information to his followers. The FBI knew the Branch Davidians listened to the daily press briefings on transistor radios, so the briefings were used by negotiators as a way of communicating with Koresh and of keeping people inside the compound informed. SAC Robert Ricks was placed in charge of press briefings.

On March 8 and 9 at the FBI's request, the Branch Davidians made a videotape of themselves. Schneider was the videographer. On the video, members record their thoughts on the raid, life at Mount Carmel and their personal feelings about being part of the sect. An injured Koresh, unshaven and dressed in a white, sleeveless tee shirt speaks to the camera with some of his children calmly sitting on his lap. "This is my family, and nobody is going to come in on top of my family and start pushing my family around," he says. He shows the bullet wounds he received during the February 28 raid. While filming, Schneider also served as interviewer and asked the residents how they came to be students of Koresh's at Mount Carmel Center. Each in his or her own words tells of acceptance of Koresh and the messages he translates from the Bible.

Afraid of public sympathy swinging to the side of the Davidians, the Justice Department made the decision not to release the tape. Seeing the residents in their own home and hearing them describe their faith in their own words took some the public's perception of the sect's mystery out of the equation, and made them appear ordinary and human, almost as if they could be next door neighbors.

In this April 15, 1993 photo, floodlights pierce through the sky behind the Branch Davidian Compound.

By the middle of March the FBI had begun to use psychological warfare to get the Branch Davidians to surrender. Powerful spotlights were shined on the compound after dark to deprive the residents of sleep. Recordings of everything from Nancy Sinatra's '60's hit song "These Boots are Made for Walkin'," to sirens, Tibetan chants, Christmas songs, and the sounds of rabbits being slaughtered were broadcast over a PA system. Helicopters flew overhead at all hours.

Some of the FBI negotiators disagreed with the psychological tactics used against the Branch Davidians, and felt them to be counter-productive and weaken the credibility of the negotiators.

In attempt to urge surrender, Sage began bypassing Koresh and speaking directly to the residents over a loudspeaker. The FBI played messages telling of fair treatment by those who had left the compound. Audiotapes of relatives' messages to the residents were also played.

Schneider and Koresh were given several deadlines by which to send people out of the compound. When they were ignored, armored vehicles cleared away cars, go-carts, trees, fences, and other obstruction from the building's exterior. At one point a tank ran over the telephone line, severing it. The residents hung out a sign that read: "Tanks Broke Phone Line," to let the negotiators know they had no means of communicating with them.

Schneider was repeatedly challenged to take responsibility for the residents and lead them out of the building. By doing so, the negotiators tried to develop animosity between Koresh and Schneider, but Schneider remained loyal to Koresh. Schneider was becoming more antagonistic with negotiators, accusing them several times of wanting to burn down the building and "get rid of the evidence."

On March 11 as the Branch Davidians were listening to Paul Harvey's radio show on their transistor radios, they heard him refer to an approaching comet as a "guitar shaped nebula." Koresh believed this to be one of the signs from God he had been awaiting. The fact that the comet was guitar shaped further reinforced Koresh's belief that this was a sign, as he had frequently used his rock band to advance his mission as a prophet. However, in subsequent conversations, Koresh denied this was the sign from God he had been searching for.

Throughout the standoff, the FBI had difficulty maintaining the perimeter of the compound. On two occasions, individuals unrelated and unknown to the Branch Davidians managed to enter the building. Both left Mount Carmel before April 19.

In late March, Dick DeGuerin, a well-known Texan criminal defense attorney, became Koresh's counsel. Between March 29 and April 4, DeGuerin and Schneider's attorney, Jack Zimmerman visited Mount Carmel five times to assist with negotiations. By the middle of April, however, Koresh was taking calls from no one, not even his own lawyer.

On March 22 a new negotiation strategy was presented to Koresh and Schneider in the form of letter sent by Jamar. The offers allowed Koresh to communicate with his congregates, as well as hold religious services while in jail. Korsesh would also be allowed to make another worldwide broadcast. Koresh told the investigators that he wasn't happy with the offer and discarded the letter. The next morning, the FBI read the letter over the loudspeaker for all the residents to hear. One Koreshan, Livingstone Fagan, came out, stating Koresh had sent him out to be the group's spokesman.

Although Koresh told the negotiators on March 28 he did not intend to die in the compound, the FBI was becoming increasingly impatient with Koresh's delays. In early April, Koresh informed the authorities the residents would come out after Passover, which they were planning to celebrate between April 7 and 14. During Passover Koresh wrote and delivered the first of five letters to the FBI. The letter threatened a natural disaster to Waco if the authorities interfered with Koresh's life mission. The letter read in part: "Learn from David My Seals or, as you have said, bear the consequences. I forewarn you the Lake Waco area of

In the first of five letters from David Koresh to the FBI, Koresh threatens that "the Lake Waco area and old Mount Carmel will be terribly shaken."

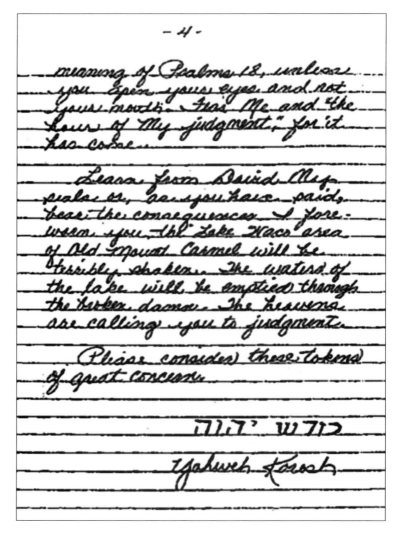

Old Mount Carmel will be terribly shaken. The waters of the lake will be emptied through the broken damn [*sic*]. The heavens are calling you to judgment. Please consider these tokens of great concern." It was signed "Yahweh Koresh." The FBI feared a Koresh sympathizer might blow up a dam to make his prophecy come true.

The FBI consulted with experts in an effort to better understand Koresh, but received contradictory opinions. Some experts felt Koresh was possibly a functioning paranoid psychotic who had no intention of surrendering. Another expert suggested it was possible Koresh was suffering from a seizure disorder. Professor Parks Dietz, professor of psychiatry and behavioral sciences at UCLA Medical School, arrived in Waco on March 2, and was given 1,000 pages of background material to read on Koresh and the Branch Davidians. His memorandum would be consulted for the remainder of the siege. He saw Koresh as a psychopath to whom appeals to the rational side of his personality would lead to failure. Dr. Dietz also felt Koresh had antisocial and narcissistic traits that made him "a master at manipulation." Dr. Dietz did not do an in-person evaluation to reach his conclusions. Dr. Giovanni, another psychiatrist consulted by the FBI, reviewed negotiation transcript and the videotape. He found no evidence of psychosis in Koresh and found his religious beliefs were not delusional, but well grounded in religious faith. The inconsistencies in the advice of the experts further frustrated the FBI's theories on how to deal with Koresh.

Via radio broadcasts that they knew the residents listened to, Biblical scholars Phillip Arnold and James D. Tabor were able to communicate to Koresh their understanding of his interpretations. They offered to help the FBI interpret the Biblical passages to which Koresh was referring from the Branch Davidian point of view.

Based upon their talks with Fagan, who had an education in theology, Koresh would accept any outcome of the siege that God wanted. In a book Tabor co-authored with Eugene V. Gallagher, he says: "Fagan had stressed the outcome of the crisis was completely open-ended and undetermined . . . what would transpire depended on how the government authorities responded to Koresh's efforts to communicate his biblical faith. The Mount Carmel siege was a spiritual test for our culture to determine whether or not we would listen to God's final messenger."

Just after the eight-day Passover celebrations, Koresh revealed in a letter to his attorney a communication from God in which he received an assignment to write the decoded message of the Seven Seals. "I hope to finish this as soon as possible, and to stand before man to answer any and all questions regarding my actions," Koresh states in his letter which again he signed "Yahweh Koresh." Koresh immediately began writing, and by Sunday, April 18, the day before the inferno, he had completed an essay on the First Seal and was busy at work on the Second.

The negotiators saw Koresh's need to write about the Seven Seals as going back on his word and not keeping his promises to surrender. They joked about this latest delay tactic and asked if they would next have to wait until he had written his memoirs. According to Tabor and Gallagher, however, after Koresh reneged on his initial intention to surrender on March 2, his stance remained the same throughout the siege. He had been told to wait, and he would wait, until he received permission from God to leave.

By April 13 when Koresh came to the telephone to speak to negotiators, his conversations were rambling religious sermons that lasted hours. He called himself "Christ" and the "Lord." Negotiators referred to his conversation as "Bible Babble." At times Koresh would be so persistent in his preaching that the negotiators could not interrupt him to speak about the surrender.

According to Tabor and Gallagher, Koresh desperately wanted the FBI to recognize his scriptural wisdom. What the negotiators didn't understand was that surrender could only be arranged through dialog within the Biblical framework in which the Branch Davidians lived.

Janet Reno, concerned about the allegations of child abuse at the Branch Davidian Compound, approved the use of CS gas because she was informed by her advisors that it wouldn't be permanently harmful or start a fire. Her offer to resign after the disaster was rejected by President Clinton.

The FBI began making plans for a tear gas assault on the Branch Davidians in late March. According to the U.S. Department of Justice's *Report to the Deputy Attorney General on the Events at Waco, Texas,* newly sworn in Attorney General Janet Reno was advised there was an impasse in the negotiations. She also understood from her advisors that the threat of child abuse continued in the compound during negotiations, an allegation that was misleading and never corroborated. Reno was not informed that Koresh was at work writing about the

Seven Seals and that he had promised to surrender after he completed his essays.

While the safety of the children was her first concern, the extreme difficulty in maintaining a safe and secure perimeter around the compound, the risk of disease caused by deteriorating sanitary conditions, the remaining Branch Davidians' refusal to leave any time in the foreseeable future, and the large amounts of food and water the residents had stockpiled also had a part in Reno's decision to approve a plan to tear gas the compound. The strategy was to inject tear gas into the building over a period of two days, a tactic that held the promise of forcing the Koreshans out of Mount Carmel.

The tear gas to be used was orthochlorobenzalmalononitrile (abbreviated CS) gas. It is a white powder that causes the eyes to tear upon contact. The United States along with 100 other nations have banned its use in warfare. CS gas is known to cause death when used in poorly ventilated areas. Excessive exposure to the gas may affect the nervous system to such an extent as to make it impossible to vacate an area. In addition, according to manufacturer's guidelines, when CS gas is burned, it releases lethal fumes.

Reno held a meeting on April 12 with senior officials of the Department of Justice and the FBI to discuss the plan to gas the compound. Reno was particularly appalled by the lack of sanitary conditions to which the children were subjected. In an interview on CNN, Reno said, "If I delayed, without sanitation or toilets there . . . I could go in there in two months and find children dead from any number of things."

Reno wouldn't give her approval to the plan unless she was confident it would not harm pregnant women and young children. Reno was assured by Dr. Harry Salem of the Edgewood Research Development and

Engineering Center in Maryland and others that the CS gas was non-lethal, wouldn't permanently harm adults or children, and wouldn't start a fire during delivery. It was also the unanimous opinion of the experts that gassing the compound was the best way to prevent mass suicide because the gas would disorient anyone trying to kill themselves or others.

Reno countered with a strategy of her own: why not let the residents run out of water? The FBI argued that with careful rationing, the siege could go on indefinitely. Reno was also concerned about the possibility of explosion. The FBI provided answers to all of the Attorney General's questions. Still, Reno would not give her consent and requested a documented statement discussing the situation inside of the compound, the progress of the negotiations, and the merits of the proposed plan. Satisfied that the "documentation was there," on Saturday, April 17, Reno gave her approval for the assault on Mount Carmel. Written into the plan was a clause allowing the assault to escalate if the tanks were fired upon.

On Sunday, April 18, Reno called President Clinton to inform him of her decision. The President offered his support for the plan. "I said that if she thought it was the right thing to do, that she should proceed, and that I would support it," President Clinton explained after the fire. Reno assured him the tear gas would be delivered incrementally over 48 hours. "April 19 is not D-Day," she told the President.

The same day, in anticipation of the insertion of the gas, armored vehicles began removing Branch Davidians' automobiles from the front of the compound. The cars had been used by ATF agents as cover during the raid on February 28. Removing them now to make room for the Combat Engineering Vehicles (CEVs) that would insert tear gas into the compound destroyed evidence.

A sniper reported to his commander that during the clearing operation, he observed a cardboard sign with the words "flames await" placed in a compound window. The sign also had flames drawn on it.

Before dawn on the morning of April 19, a phone call was made to the compound by Chief Negotiator Sage. Reaching Schneider, the conversation was simultaneously broadcasted over the public address system for all the Mount Carmel residents to hear.

"There's going to be tear gas injected into the compound," said Sage. "This is not an assault. Do not fire. The idea is to get you out of the compound." They told the Davidians exactly where the tear gas would be injected so the children could be moved away. The tear gas was introduced at both ends of the building so as to force the occupants out the front door.

Many residents were still sleeping; and those who were awake were reading their Bibles. According to survivors, the adults put on gas masks and covered the faces of the children with wet blankets and towels.

The message over the loudspeaker warned residents to come out, that they were under arrest. "David, you have had your 15 minutes of fame . . . leave the building now . . . you are all under arrest . . . the stand off is over. . . . "

One hundred seventy FBI agents surrounded Mount Carmel as Combat Engineering Vehicles began punching holes into the building and injecting CS gas through spray nozzles attached to their booms. The CS gas was suspended in methylene chloride, a highly combustible petroleum derivative.

The FBI claims the residents shot at the tanks, a claim the Koreshans deny. The FBI assault force then began firing dozens of "ferret rounds" (canisters of CS gas) into the building.

The tanks knocked down walls and the staircases,

making it impossible to exit the building. Three dozen women and children seeking protection in the concrete walk-in cooler were crushed and suffocated by falling concrete.

At approximately 12:10 in the afternoon, smoke was seen coming from the second floor on the right side of building, and shortly thereafter from the backside of the building near kitchen. Fanned by 30 mph winds, the building quickly became a raging inferno. SSRA Sage continued to repeat his message while the building burned. According to the FBI, fire-fighting equipment had not been put on standby at the compound during the

On April 19, 1993, an armored vehicle drives by the Branch Davidian Compound. The compound exploded into flames just after noon.

assault due to safety concerns. The Branch Davidians were known to have .50 caliber weapons which are capable of firing 3,000 yards.

The origin of the fire has been widely debated. The FBI had a fixed-wing aircraft equipped with forward-looking infrared radar (FLIR) in the air above Mount Carmel to detect fire. Theories range from Koresh's setting the fire himself, to the ignition of Malotov cocktails being thrown at the invading tanks, to a lantern being knocked over by residents during the confusion. HRT observers claim they saw a male inside the compound start the fire. One survivor recalls hearing someone say, "Light the fire," but this is contradicted by other survivors who state that tanks crashing into Mount Carmel knocked over lanterns and cans of fuel, including propane gas which the residents were using for heating and cooking.

As viewers all over the world watched on TVs in their living rooms, the raging fire quickly consumed Mount Carmel killing 82 Branch Branch Davidians, including 25 children under the age of 15. Nine residents survived the fire.

Agents reported hearing gunfire coming from the burning compound and believed the Branch Davidians were either killing themselves or one another. Autopsies later showed that Koresh, Schneider, and several other Branch Davidians were killed by gunshots to the head. Koresh's body showed evidence of a bullet entrance mid-forehead area, about an inch above the brow that exited out the back of his head, near the top. Federal agents claimed Koresh committed suicide or asked someone to murder him. His badly burned body yielded no clues as to how close the gun had been to his head when it had been fired. Survivors believe either ATF or FBI agents shot Koresh. Without the presence or absence of powder burn evidence, it was impossible to tell.

Accepting full responsibility for the disaster Reno told CNN of her decision, "It was based on what we knew then. Based upon what we know now, it was obviously wrong."

In another news conference Reno stated, "I approved the plan and I'm responsible for it. I advised the President, but I did not advise him to the details." Following the Mount Carmel inferno, Attorney General Reno offered President Clinton her resignation, which he declined.

Throughout the siege, David Koresh and the Branch Davidians believed they were living the fifth seal of the Book of Revelation and could quite possibly be killed at Mount Carmel. After the inferno, ATF called in an arson team assembled from experts from throughout the country to study the fire and determine its origin. The team concluded that the fire had been started in three different places inside the compound by the Branch Davidians themselves, and not by the FBI. The study further showed that the Branch Davidians could have escaped the fire if they had wanted. It appeared as if the Branch Davidians had purposely orchestrated their deaths to prove to the world the accuracy of their prophecy.

What Went Wrong at Waco?

The Branch Davidian Compound was engulfed in flames. Among the victims killed in the fire were 25 children under the age of 15.

5

The 51-day siege at Mount Carmel was unparalleled in the history of American civilian law enforcement and the largest law enforcement effort ever conducted by ATF. Never before had such a unified group armed themselves so heavily and barricaded themselves in direct defiance of recognized law enforcement officials attempting to serve a federal warrant.

The cost of federal and local law enforcement involvement with the Branch Davidians ran into millions of dollars. Over 700 federal, state, and local agents worked around the clock to end the siege. Personnel from ATF, FBI, United States Customs, the Waco Police Department, McLennan County Sheriff's Office, the Texas Department of Public Safety, the United States Army, and the Texas National

Guard participated during the seven-week standoff.

In the aftermath of the February 28 raid, the subsequent standoff and the culmination of events on April 19, the president, Congress, the media, and the general public raised serious questions about ATF and FBI action at Mount Carmel and the roles the agencies played in the deaths of the Branch Davidians. President Clinton instructed the Department of the Treasury and the Department of Justice to conduct a "vigorous and thorough" investigation. Three separate inquiries were undertaken late April 1993. At the request of Secretary of the Treasury Lloyd Bentsen, the Treasury Department studied ATF's involvement from its initial investigation of David Koresh through the raid on February 28. Attorney General Janet Reno directed Deputy Attorney General Philip B. Heymann to review the FBI involvement from March 1, when the HRT took over, until April 19. A third inquiry directed by Reno was a joint study of the United States law enforcement's ability to handle the dangerous situations encountered when an attempt was made to serve the search and arrest warrants on February 28.

The goal of the Treasury Department's study was to determine whether ATF's "procedures, policies and practices were adequate, and whether they were followed." Secretary Bentson appointed three individuals with extensive expertise in law enforcement and media relations to oversee the investigations. They did so *pro bono* (without monetary compensation). The reviewers had access to all data collected during the investigations, and were free to ask for additional inquiries or to conduct them on their own. Altogether, 508 individuals were interviewed between May and September 1993. The Department of Justice conducted a simultaneous investigation into the criminal violations of the Branch

Davidians and a redacted (edited or censored) version of this investigation was published in October 1993.

The Treasury Department's investigation confirmed that the rank and file agents of ATF sent to enforce federal firearms and explosives laws at the Branch Davidian Compound did their best to perform their assigned tasks, and showed dedication and courage in the face of murderous gunfire. Additionally, the investigation found disturbing evidence of flawed decision making, inadequate intelligence gathering, miscommunication, supervisory failures, and deliberately misleading post-raid statements about the raid and the raid plan by certain ATF supervisors. The Justice Report, while more favorable than the Treasury Report, found inconsistencies with the information provided to Attorney General Reno, especially on the subject of child abuse.

The Office of the Assistant Secretary for Enforcement oversees the Bureau of Alcohol, Tobacco and Firearms. Because there was no guideline in place at the time requiring the office to be notified by ATF prior to an operation, it was not advised of the plans to assault Mount Carmel until 48 hours prior to the raid. This left little opportunity for the Office of Enforcement to review or evaluate ATF's planned strategies. Since the Mount Carmel siege, new guidelines have been put in place to allow the Office for Enforcement time for adequate review and evaluation of ATF plans.

The findings of the Treasury Department Report showed the ATF commanders' decision to proceed with the raid knowing it had been compromised was a wrong one. The decision to move forward with the raid demonstrated, in addition to bad judgment, a deficiency in intelligence gathering and processing, poor strategic planning and personnel decisions, and a general failure of ATF management to abort the raid, knowing the Branch Davidians had been tipped off.

The Treasury Report concluded that in the aftermath of the February 28 raid, ATF lacked the planning, training, and resources to accomplish the following:

- provide prompt medical attention to wounded agents or have a plan in place for the removal of ATF casualties

- withdraw safely from vulnerable positions inside the compound

- establish and maintain a secure perimeter around the compound to prevent escape of adult residents

- evacuate residents who wished to leave the compound, especially children

- provide the public with information about the raid

The Treasury Review also found the decision to execute the warrants by raiding the compound was made before other options were fully exhausted. One alternative that should have been more fully explored was to lure Koresh away from the compound and arrest him off site. According to ATF Intelligence Chief David Troy, Koresh did not leave the compound after an arrest warrant was issued on February 23. However, Koresh was known to leave Mount Carmel to conduct business in town often, and would have most likely left Mount Carmel sooner or later, providing an opportunity to arrest him away from his followers. ATF raised the concern that if Koresh was arrested, the Branch Davidians might start executing their own members until he was released. This was conjecture with no fact to back it up. To serve the warrants on a heavily armed group of people such as the Branch Davidians, ATF determined they needed the element

Under the U.S. flag, the Texas flag and the ATF flag hang over the site where the Branch Davidian Compound once stood.

of surprise, and did not adequately study other means of serving the warrants.

The possibility of mass suicide deterred the planners from considering the less risky siege option. The Treasury report suggested the planners should have sought the assistance of psychologists and other experts equipped to evaluate the accounts of former Branch Davidians to improve ATF's overall understanding of Koresh and his followers prior to the February 28 raid. The experts should have included those familiar with the group dynamics of cult members and, in particular, those able to interpret and explain the extraordinary beliefs of the Branch Davidians. Such an understanding may have allowed ATF to better understand the group's theories regarding an apocalypse, leading to the consideration of other law enforcement options.

Intelligence failure was assigned partial blame for the unsuccessful outcome of the raid. Intelligence inconsistent with the assumptions of the raid leaders was discarded instead of investigated. One example of this was when former cult member, David Block, told ATF the weapons were kept under lock and key in the gun room next to Koresh's bedroom, ATF's treated the report as fact without further investigation. The planners disregarded Block's additional reports that guns were sometimes stored under beds, and that members of the compound participated in frequent target practices. After the fire, arms were found stored in other locations in the compound in addition to the arms room.

Most raids are conducted pre-dawn when people are likely to be asleep. ATF based its decision to conduct a 10:00 A.M. raid because it was believed the men would be unarmed and working in the construction pit. This was based upon false information provided by ATF's own undercover agents living in the undercover house across from Mount Carmel. The agents had ceased around the clock surveillance of Mount Carmel on February 17. Furthermore, the entrance to the construction pit wasn't easily visible from the undercover house, making it difficult to see the comings and goings of the workers. A review of the surveillance logs from the undercover house, show the Branch Davidians worked in the construction pit only 14 out of 36 days prior to the raid. When it rained, or there was water in the construction pit as was the case on February 28, the men were unable to work. The raid planners based their entire strategy on the assumption the men would be working in the construction pit. None of the raid commanders checked out the construction pit to see if and how many Koreshans were there working before going forward with the raid.

Other areas of inaccurate intelligence caused the raid planners to overlook the possibility of the women also being armed, and the presence of armed sentries guarding the compound.

The reviewers found the raid plan had no contingency for the possibility the Branch Davidians would be forewarned and the loss of the element of surprise. There was no contingency plan in place in the event ATF agents were met with an organized ambush or pockets of resistance. Neither was there a plan to peacefully serve the warrants.

The review found Incident Commander Phil Chojnacki and Tactical Coordinator Charles Sarabyn to be ill-prepared by training and experience for the command of a high-risk assault of the magnitude required for a large, heavily armed structure such as the Branch Davidian Compound. The National Response Plan specified a command structure for major operations, and the plan assigns critical command positions based upon rank, not ability, experience, training, or knowledge of the case. Because Chojnacki was the special agent in charge for the affected ATF field division, the NRP specified that he serve as Incident Commander for the raid, regardless of whether he had adequate tactical training and experience. Chojnacki chose Charles Sarabyn to be tactical coordinator, despite his lack of large-scale tactical planning experience. Neither Chojnacki nor Sarabyn had experience comparable to the raid attempted on February 28. Neither had trained

In this September 1999 photo, some faded words can be read at the site of the unfinished swimming pool at the Branch Davidian Compound.

in operations of this magnitude or had relevant military tactical experience that might have compensated for that lack. In addition, the command and control plan written for the raid failed to place commanders where they could make informed decisions and maintain control over the events. Chojnacki was in a helicopter and could not effectively communicate with other raid commanders or the SRT team. Sarabyn was riding with the cattle trailers, severely limiting his ability to receive and process information. The only commander placed at a vantage point that allowed him to maintain perspective over the operation was Special Agent James Cavanaugh, who was located in the undercover house.

Upon learning that the *Waco Tribune-Herald* was preparing to publish the "Sinful Messiah" series, Sarabyn asked Managing Editor Barbara Elmore to delay publication until ATF had completed its investigation. The ATF was understandably concerned that publication of the series could alert Koresh that some sort of enforcement action was imminent. In subsequent meetings with the *Waco Tribune-Herald* management, Sarabyn and Chojnacki not only disclosed ATF's plans to arrest Koresh, but also the approximate date of the raid. Members of the review team questioned whether alerting the press to the raid and its approximate date showed good judgment. The same men planning to carry it out may very well have violated the operational security of the raid on the Branch Davidians.

On March 1 consistent with ATF policy, a "shooting review" team was created to study the Branch Davidian raid with special attention to the firefight. During the investigation, Sarabyn and Chojnacki gave misleading and false information regarding their conversations with Rodriquez, the undercover agent who was in the compound at the time Koresh received the warning. Rodriquez and other witnesses testified to having told the commanders that Koresh knew they were on their way, yet Sarabyn and Chojnacki testified they either did not hear Rodriquez or understand his message. Their statements were incriminating in light of the number service people who heard Sarabyn and Chojnacki hurry the agents into the cattle cars.

Mount Carmel's structure, the weapons its residents

had amassed, the loyalty and discipline of Koresh's followers, and the absence of cover around the building itself, made a direct assault against forewarned assailants unacceptably risky. Perhaps the largest unanswered question of the review was why the raid went forward when the element of surprise had knowingly been compromised. An independent review submitted as part of the Treasury Report gave the following explanations as to why the raid went forward on February 28:

- the scope and magnitude of Operation Trojan Horse was unprecedented and overwhelming

- decision-making was difficult because there was a collective lack of experience in crisis management among the raid commanders

- the large buildup of manpower and resources created an instinctive reluctance to cancel, postpone, or abort the operation

- the belief that something had to be done to resolve the continuing situation at the compound

Perhaps the most compelling reason to go ahead was that the integrity of the agency was at stake. In January, ABC's prime time television show, *60 Minutes* had aired allegations of sexual harassment within the agency. ATF hoped the raid would booster support for the agency, which was coming up coming up for budgetary considerations on March 10th. The raid was to be filmed in the air from the helicopters and also on the ground. The planning and training sessions for Operation Trojan Horse had been videotaped prior to February 28. A video showing the agents in action would speak well for the agency, exerting even more pressure on the commanders to give the go-ahead.

On March 15 a "gag order" (an order not to speak

Armaments recovered from the Branch David-ian Compound are stored by the Texas Department of Public Safety in Austin, Texas.

about the raid) was imposed upon all ATF agents. Dismissal was threatened for those who ignored it. Despite the gag order, several members of ATF granted interviews to the *New York Times,* alleging that even though the commanders knew the Koreshans had been tipped off, agents were sent into the conflict unaware the residents knew they were coming and unprepared for the amount of firepower the group possessed.

In October 1994, 20 months after the unsuccessful raid, Phillip Chojnacki and Charles Sarabyn were charged with poor judgment and lying to investigators and dismissed from ATF. Steven Higgins, a 30-year veteran of ATF who had served as director for 10 of those years, resigned. In December 1994, both Sarabyn and Chojnacki were reinstated with full back pay and benefits.

The investigations into the Waco raid also raised questions of the violations of Posse Comitatus Act, which forbids the deployment of American military forces against civilians unless they are suspected of illegal drug activity. Neither FBI nor ATF had proof the Koreshans had any involvement with drugs. However, some residents had prior drug convictions and prior to Koresh taking over, there had been a methamphetamine lab at Mount Carmel. Aquilera was able to get the use of the National Guard helicopters for the raid based upon these two pieces of information. The investigation found no violation of the Posse Comitatus Act.

In 1995 both Houses of Congress held hearings into the incident. The House met in July and the Senate in October and November. The following concerns were addressed by the congressional hearings:

1. The accusation the FBI destroyed evidence that would incriminate ATF. Throughout the siege, Koresh maintained that the first shots fired during the raid were from ATF's semiautomatic weapons that entered the building through the right-hand side of the front door. An examination of the door would have provided evidence as to the trajectory of the bullets, but during the April 19 fire, an armored vehicle steered by FBI agents disengaged the door

from the rest of the building. The door subsequently disappeared in the fire and was never found. Likewise, the bullet holes in the cars parked outside of Mount Carmel could also have provided evidence relative to the shooting, but they were destroyed by tanks in preparation for the tear-gassing.

2. The initial search warrants were based upon affidavits containing false information. The ATF agents responsible for preparing the affidavits knew or should have known that many of the statements were false. The Congressional review recommended the ATF agents be prosecuted for supplying the false information.

During the Senate Judiciary hearings in October 1995, Lisa Kaufman, a staff aide on the committee, presents photos from the 1993 siege.

3. The Senate report found the FBI's Hostage Rescue Team acted in opposition to the FBI negotiators. One incident cited the negotiators having 20 Branch Davidians ready to surrender then refusing, because loud music was played throughout the night.

4. Attorney General Reno's approval of the use of tear gas was premature. The negotiations had not reached an impasse, as she was advised. From her accounts to the media on the day of the fire, Reno stated that it was the charge of child abuse more than anything else that persuaded her to okay the tear-gassing. Later that same week, the Department of Justice clarified the unsubstantiated child abuse charges, saying they had no evidence of child abuse during the 51-day siege. The report further recommended that President Clinton should have accepted Reno's resignation.

5. The Congressional Investigation concurred with the findings of the Treasury Department and the Justice Department with respect to ATF, namely, the top level of personnel for the Treasury Department acted irresponsibly by failing to request briefings on the raid or monitor the actions of ATF. The investigation of the Branch Davidians by ATF prior to the February 28 raid was incompetent, and ATF exercised extremely poor judgement in executing a "dynamic entry" and should have arrested Koresh out side the Branch Davidian Compound.

    • Congressional representatives further found the ATF undercover surveillance operation lacked professionalism, and ATF's plan raid plan was flawed and poorly conceived. They recommended Congress consider moving ATF from the Treasury Department to the Justice Department.

- Regarding the actions of the FBI, the Congressional hearing found the FBI should have continued negotiation even if it took several more weeks, and the FBI failed to show concern for children, the elderly, and pregnant women when they inserted the tear gas.

Perhaps the biggest unanswered question about the Waco disaster is how the fire was started. There have been three theories regarding the origin of the fire. The first suggests the Koreshans started it themselves. An FBI agent testified he saw a resident on the second floor involved in a motion that could be interpreted as starting a fire. Some survivors recall hearing "the fires have been lit" during the final moments in Mount Carmel. Yet none of the survivors say they actually saw a Branch Davidian light the fire.

The second theory suggests the FBI intentionally started the fire. April 19 was a dry day with fire fanning, 30 mph winds. The water that might have been used to put out the fire was cut off. There was no fire-fighting equipment on hand. This theory suggests the FBI agents became frustrated after none of the residents came out of the building after six hours of tear-gassing.

The third theory is that the fire was started accidentally by overturned lanterns during the tear-gassing. Survivors have consistently stated that this is how the fire started. The flammability of the building and the high winds, among other factors would have insured the fire to rage out of control once it got started.

Whether the fires were intentionally or accidentally set may never be known for sure.

The House's report released July 11, 1996, put the blame for the deaths at Mount Carmel on David Koresh and the Branch Davidians. It found there was no evidence the FBI intentionally set the fire.

A memorial marker stands at the former site of the Branch Davidian Compound.

MOUNT CARMEL CENTER

On February 28, 1993 a church and its members known as Branch Davidians came under attack by ATF and FBI agents. For 51 days the Davidians and their leader, David Koresh, stood proudly. On April 19, 1993 the Davidians and their church were burned to the ground. 82 people perished during the siege. 18 were children 10 years old or younger.

The House's report also found no evidence that the FBI used gunfire on April 19, in direct opposition to testimony of survivors who said FBI agents shot into the compound as residents were attempting to flee. The Committee for Waco Justice is an organized group of citizens who continues to work towards uncovering the true story behind the Waco Massacre and bringing the truth to the American people.

Attorneys for both Koresh and Schneider believe the group would have peacefully surrendered or at the very least, more women and children would have been allowed to leave. The FBI negotiators called to Mount Carmel on February 28 were not familiar with religious groups espousing Apocalyptic theories in general, and Koresh or the Branch Davidians in particular. The Branch Davidians saw themselves as attacked in their own church without provocation; the FBI saw them as hostages of a psychopath con man suffering from delusional paranoia. The Branch Davidians saw themselves as fulfilling Biblical prophecies. To surrender on the FBI's terms was asking them to relinquish everything meaningful in their lives—their home at Mount Carmel, and their spiritual relationships with Koresh and with each other. Writing about the Seven Seals was important to Koresh and his followers; a completed manuscript meant they could come out.

The Branch Davidians believed the outcome was destined and their duty was faithfulness to God and Koresh, whom they believed to be the world's final prophet. The Branch Davidians would not have come out of Mount Carmel until they believed it was God's will to do so.

The Revenge of Waco

6

P resident Clinton defended the government's actions at Waco in a
news conference on the morning of April 20, 1993. He claimed
the April 19 assault was a way to increase pressure on those in the
compound and persuade them to peaceful surrender. "We did everything we could to avoid the loss of life," the President said. "They made
the decision to immolate themselves, and I regret it terribly, and I feel
awful about the children."

In the days and weeks following the Waco siege and inferno, it became
apparent that there was discrepancy between what the federal government
had to say about Waco and what the public believed. This led to two camps
of public opinion.

Politically moderate Americans who, despite their dislike for Koresh and his followers, were skeptical of the government's account of mass suicide. They believed Waco could have been avoided had the Branch Davidians laid down their weapons and surrendered regardless of who had fired the first shot.

A second group of Americans, the "militia movement," saw the government's actions at Waco as threatening the freedoms guaranteed by the American constitution. An informal system of paramilitary organizations, these groups seek to protect the citizens of the United States from its own federal government. The Neo-Nazis, Aryan Nations, White Supremacists, and the Christian Identity organization are a few of the groups that comprise the militia movement.

To the militia movement, the events at Waco were a repeat of another incident that had taken place at Ruby Ridge, Idaho, two years prior. Randy Weaver was a member of the Christian Identity movement, a group that believes the descendents of the Biblical figure Abraham are not the Jews, but Anglo-Saxon and other white ethnic groups.

On October 11, 1989, Weaver, at one time a candidate for Boundary County, Idaho sheriff, sold two sawed-off shotguns to an undercover ATF agent. On January 17, 1989, after refusing to provide information on the weapons involvement of other Christian Identity members, Weaver was arrested and subsequently released on a $100,000 bond. Due to confusion over a court appearance date, Weaver received a failure-to-appear warrant on February 20, 1991. He then secluded himself and his family (his wife, son, adopted son, and two daughters) on Ruby Ridge, a mountain in northern Idaho. There the family remained for the next 18 months. While living in their mountain cabin, Weaver's wife, Vicki, gave birth to a third daughter. Other members of the Christian Identity Movement brought them food and supplies. Their retreat was armed with six rifles, six revolvers, and thousands of rounds of ammunition.

On Friday, August 21, 1991, in an exchange of gunfire in the woods around the cabin, Sammy Weaver, Randy's 13-year-old son, and a United States deputy marshal were both killed. Kevin Harris, Randy Weaver's adopted son shot and killed the marshal. Later that same evening, Larry Potts, head of the criminal division of the FBI, now in charge of the case, changed the FBI rules of engagement for Ruby Ridge. Under usual circumstances, FBI agents must be provoked before firing, and whenever possible, must give verbal warning. The new command allowed ATF to kill anyone on Ruby Ridge without provocation and without warning.

On August 22, 1991, Vicki Weaver, holding her baby daughter in her arms, was killed as she opened her front porch door to allow the family, fleeing from sniper gunfire, into the cabin. Weaver, his surviving three children, and Harris remained in the cabin. During this time there was a noticeable increase in anti-government opinion. Neighbors and self-proclaimed white supremacist gathered in support of the Weavers. The standoff also received national attention.

On August 31, 1991, 11 days after Vicki Weaver's death, Randy Weaver surrendered. Bo Gritz, a decorated Vietnam War veteran Green Beret who was a prominent antigovernment activist and Christian Identity believer, accompanied him. At the time he was running for president of the United States on the Populist ticket.

Both Weaver and Harris were acquitted in the

This August 1992 photo of Randy Weaver supporters was taken at Ruby Ridge in northern Idaho.

death of the deputy marshal. Weaver was acquitted of the charges stemming from the original firearm investigation, but found guilty of failing to appear in court in 1991. Weaver's trial began on April 14, 1993. During the trial a breaking news story was taking place in Waco, Texas. The 51-day siege at the Branch Davidian Compound known as Mount Carmel had ended in an inferno that had taken the lives of David Koresh and 81 of his followers.

The events at Waco and Ruby Ridge caused many Americans to come to the conclusion that the American government is dangerous. Immediately after both incidents, thousands of United States citizens joined anti-government militia organizations. "April 19" became the battle cry for the paramilitary groups of the United States. The Second Amendment to the

Constitution: *A well-regulated militia being necessary to the security of a free state, the right of the people to keep and bear arms shall not be infringed* became their motto.

The similarities between Ruby Ridge and Waco were obvious. In both situations, shoot-outs and sieges had been the result of the government's attempt to serve a search warrant for suspected firearms violations. However, the leaders of the American militia movement argued because the Branch Davidians had no illegal weapons, they had not committed a crime. Once fired upon, they had the constitutional right to defend themselves against the United States government.

The Waco allies argued that the Branch Davidians were the victims of unprovoked aggression by the United States government. They pointed out the bulldozing of Mount Carmel, which covered up the signs of the helicopter attack on the roof and walls, the evidence of which would have most probably allowed the Branch Davidians to be acquitted. They claimed ATF and FBI entered into conspiracy to sabotage negotiations with Koresh by withholding from Attorney General Reno that Koresh was writing the Seven Seals. They felt betrayed by the Clinton Administration because no ATF or FBI agent was ever punished for Waco, Texas, yet surviving Branch Davidians were punished for defending themselves against an ATF assault.

Throughout the 51-day siege, anti-government activists had been gathering at Waco to protest the government's interference in the lives of the Branch Davidians. They held up signs and passed out anti-government leaflets and bumper stickers. One disenchanted army veteran traveled from Florida to Texas to stand in support of the people at Mount Carmel. His name was Timothy McVeigh.

The ruins of the Alfred P. Murrah Building in Oklahoma City, Oklahoma, was the result of a terrorist attack on April 19, 1995. Timothy McVeigh, executed on June 11, 2001, stated he bombed the building to avenge the dead Branch Davidians.

McVeigh was enraged by the actions at Waco. It wasn't enough to hand out pamphlets and bumper stickers; he needed to back his anti-government sentiments with firepower. On April 19, 1995, two years to the day after the Waco inferno, McVeigh committed one of the worst acts of terrorism ever committed on United States soil when he bombed the Alfred P. Murrah Building in Oklahoma City, Oklahoma. One hundred and sixty-eight people were killed, including 19 children; and over 500 people were injured. An FBI affidavit filed in the Oklahoma City federal district court stated that McVeigh was "extremely agitated" about the federal government's assault on the Branch Davidian compound near Waco, Texas. Federal prosecutors began to build a case against McVeigh based upon his two visits to Waco and his deep-seated resentment against the government. Were it not for the raid at Waco, Texas, according to the affidavit, there would have been no motive for the Oklahoma City bombing.

Ray Jahn, one of two federal prosecuting attorneys, had been involved in the raid. He is on his way to the federal courthouse in San Antonio in this January 1994 photo.

Mount Carmel Today

Eleven Branch Davidians were tried in January and February of 1994 on charges ranging from conspiracy to murder of federal agents, and various weapons charges. All 11 were found innocent of conspiracy to murder. Five were convicted of aiding and abetting voluntary manslaughter, and eight were convicted of weapons charges. One Branch Davidian received a reduced sentence of three years for cooperating with federal authorities.

The two federal prosecutors, Ray Jahn and William Johnston, had themselves been involved in the raid. The U.S. District Judge Walter J. Smith, who presided over the trial, was under investigation during the trial for lying allegedly under oath during a civil trial.

Under common law, the armed attack by the AFT gave the defendants the right to use armed force in self-defense. The judge, however, would not allow defense attorneys to mention self-defense, except in their closing arguments.

Despite this, jurors found all Branch Davidians innocent of conspiracy to murder and murder charges. The jurors were convinced the Branch Davidians acted in self-defense, and they did not find the Branch Davidians responsible for the April 19, 1993 fire.

Judge Smith did not instruct the jury that they could also find the defendants innocent of the charge of aiding and abetting voluntary manslaughter by reason of self-defense. The jurors later admitted they would have done so had they been properly instructed. At sentencing, Judge Smith stated that because the government alleged machine guns were found on the premises—the defendants carried them—despite no such finding of guilt by the jury. Eight Branch Davidians received individual prison sentences ranging from 3 to 30 years.

In January 1996, six of the convicted Branch Davidians appealed their sentences. In August of the same year the Fifth Circuit Court of Appeals upheld the convictions. Attorneys immediately filed appeals with the Supreme Court. In January 2000 the Supreme Court heard the cases and ruled to cut 25 years from four Branch Davidians' sentences and five years from one. Additionally, Livingstone Fagan, who had not appealed his sentence in protest, received 25 years off of his sentence, as well.

New policies and procedures put into effect by the FBI after Waco were used in 1996, when members of the "Freeman," an anti-government, white separtist group barricaded themselves on a 960-acre ranch in Billings, Montana. Calling their community "Justus Township," the community refused to acknowledge any government but their own. The heavily armed group set up their own police force, courts, and laws. They refused to pay income

taxes or renew their drivers' licenses. The range upon which they barricaded themselves had been foreclosed upon 18 months prior. Using the new FBI policies implement in the aftermath of Waco, the FBI patiently negotiated without provoking a confrontation. "The FBI has gone to great pains to ensure that there is no armed confrontation, no siege, no armed perimeter, and no use of military assault-type tactics or equipment," said Attorney General Janet Reno. The month-long standoff ended peacefully. Waco's lessons had been learned.

After the February 1993 raid and April 19, 1993 fire, the surviving Branch Davidians scattered. Twenty children were sent to live with relatives or placed in foster homes; two dozen mostly elderly adults were

A one-room chapel is now located at the site of the Branch Davidian Compound.

scattered across Waco or across the county or the world; 11 adults were incarcerated and tried, eight convicted. Today seven remain in prison.

Each April 19 a memorial service is held in Waco to honor the 82 Branch Davidians killed during the raid and fire. The solemn tributes to those who died are emphasized by the 82 crepe myrtle trees that stand starkly against the Texas plain, one tree in memory of each person who died.

Siege survivor Clive Jones, one of those acquitted, organized a few remaining Branch Davidians and together, with the help of volunteers, created a museum and a new church on the property where Mount Carmel once stood. Each year at the memorial service, a bell is rung 82 times. The bell sits above a sign that reads: "We Will Not Forget What Happened Here."

Chronology

1831	William Miller begins studying the Bible
1833	William Miller begins preaching his message that the end of the world will happen in 1843
1843	Miller revises his date to 1844
1844	The Second Coming of Christ does not happen on October 23; this date becomes known as the "Day of Great Disappointment"; Miller's followers lose heart
1863	The General Conference of the Seventh Day Adventist Church, under the direction of Sister Ellen G. White, is organized
1930	Victor Houteff is dismissed from the Seventh Day Adventist Church
1934	Victor Houteff forms the Davidian Seventh Day Adventists and moves to Mount Carmel, Texas
1955	Victor Houteff dies; Florence Houteff takes over the sect and predicts "End Time" for April 22, 1959; Ben Roden begins Branch Davidians Seventh Day Association
1959	Florence Houteff's prediction does not come to pass; Davidians Seventh Day Adventist organization begins to disband; Vernon Howell is born on August 17
1962-1977	Ben Roden leads the Branch Davidians
1977	Ben Roden's wife, Lois, has a vision from God and proclaims the Holy Spirit is feminine
1978	Ben Roden dies and Lois Roden becomes the leader of the Branch Davidians; she changes the name to Living Waters Branch Davidians
1978-1983	Lois heads Living Waters Branch Davidians
1980	Vernon Howell arrives at Mount Carmel; Lois is removed from Seventh Day Adventist Church
1983	Vernon Howell begins having visions which he feels are divinely inspired

Chronology

1984	George Roden forces Vernon Howell out of Mount Carmel; Vernon Howell marries Rachel Jones; Vernon Howell settles in Palestine, Texas, with a handful of followers
1985	Vernon Howell travels to Israel and receives vision that he is the Lamb of God and the one chosen to interpret the Seven Seals; he receives a vision that "End Time" would occur in 1995; Vernon Howell's official ministry begins
1986	Lois Roden dies; Vernon Howell and George Roden both claim to be leaders of the sect
1987	Vernon Howell and George Roden shoot it out over possession of Mount Carmel; Vernon Howell is arrested
1988	Vernon Howell is acquitted and all charges dropped; George Roden is imprisoned on unrelated charges; Vernon Howell moves back to Mount Carmel
1990	Vernon Howell changes his name to David Koresh; Marc Breault returns to Waco to alert authorities about illegal activities at Mount Carmel
1992	Australia's TV show, *A Current Affair*, conducts interviews with Vernon Howell; the *Waco Herald-Tribune* begins research for "The Sinful Messiah" series; ATF investigation begins
1993	ATF launches raid against Branch Davidians on February 28; Branch Davidians barricade themselves at Mount Carmel surrounded by 700 federal and local law officers until April 18; Branch Davidian Compound becomes a raging inferno on April 19 as combat vehicles driven by FBI agents send tear gas into the building; 76 people are killed
1995	Senate Judiciary hearings are held to investigate the Waco siege. Among other findings, the Judiciary committee concluded that the ATF exercised extremely poor judgment in executing a "dynamic entry" and should have arrested Koresh outside the compound.

Further Reading

Andryszewski, Tricia. *The Militia Movement in America: Before and After Oklahoma City.* Millbrook Press, 1997.

Chiles, James R. *Inviting Disaster: Lessons From the Edge of Technology.* Harperinformation, 2001.

Cole, Michael. *The Siege at Waco: Deadly Inferno (American Disasters).* Berkeley Heights, New Jersey: Enslow Publishers, 1999.

Garner, Joe. *We Interrupt This Broadcast: The Actual Broadcasts of the Events that Stopped Our Lives.* Sourcebooks, Inc. 1998.

Sherrow, Victoria. *The Oklahoma City Bombing: Terror in the Heartland (American Disasters).* Berkeley Heights, New Jersey: Enslow Publishers, 1998.

Bibliography

Books

Breault, Marc and Martin King. *Inside the Cult*. New York: Penguin, 1993.

Hamm, Mark S. *Apocalypse in Oklahoma: Waco and Ruby Ridge Revenged*. Northeastern University Press, 1997.

Lewis, James R. *From the Ashes: Making Sense of Waco*. Lanham: Rowman and Littlefield, 1994.

Linedecker, Clifford L. *Massacre At Waco, Texas*. New York: St. Martin's Press, 1993.

Michel, Lou and Dan Herbeck. *American Terrorist: Timothy McVeigh and the Oklahoma City Bombing*. New York: HarperCollins, 2001

Reavis, Dick J. *The Ashes of Waco: An Investigation*. New York: Simon and Shuster, 1995.

Singer, Margaret Thaler. *Cults in Our Midst*. Jossey-Bass Books, 1995.

Tabor, James D. and Eugene V. Gallagher. *Why Waco? Cults and the Battle for Religious Freedom in America*. Los Angeles: University of California Press, 1995.

Thibodeau, David and Leon Whiteson. *A Place Called Waco: A Survivors's Story*. New York: Publicaffairs, 1999.

Walter, Jess. *Every Knee Shall Bow: The Truth and Tragedy of Ruby Ridge and the Randy Weaver Family*. New York, HarperCollins, 1995.

Wecht, Cyril, H. *Grave Secrets*. New York: Penguin Books, 1996.

Wright, Stuart A. *Armageddon in Waco*. Chicago: University of Chicago Press, 1995.

U.S. Department of Justice, Report to the Deputy Attorney General on the Events at Waco, Texas, February to April 19, 1993. October 1993.

U.S. Department of the Treasury, Report on the Bureau of Alcohol, Tobacco and Firearms, Investigation of Vernon Wayne Howell, aka David Koresh. September 1993.

Bibliography

Articles

Beck, Melinda et. al. "The Book of Koresh." *Newsweek* 122 (October 11, 1993).

Chua-Eoan, Howard. "Tripped Up By Lies." *Time* 142: 39-40 (October 11, 1993).

Church, George J. "The End Is Near?" *Time* 142: 32 (April 26, 1993).

Harrary, Keith. "The Truth About Jonestown." *Psychology Today* 25: 62-69 (March 1992).

Kantrowitz, Barbara et. al. "Day of Judgement: How the Cult Standoff with the FBI Escalated Into a Fiery Finale." *Newsweek* (May 3, 1993).

Labaton, Stephen. "U.S. Agents Say Fatal Flaws Doomed Raid on Waco Cult." *New York Times* (March 28, 1993).

Lacayo, Richard. "Cult of Death." *Time* 122 (March 28, 1993).

Witkin, George. "How David Koresh Got All Those Guns." *U.S. News & World Report* 14: 42-43 (July 7, 1993).

Websites

Kelley, Dean M. "Waco: A Massacre and Its Aftermath." First Things, 53: 22-37 (May 1995)
[www.FirstThings.com]

Null, Gary. "Holocaust at Waco."
[http://virtualschool.edu/mon/SocialConstruction/HolocaustAtWaco.com]

ATF Website:
[http://www.atf.treas.gov/about/history.html]

Carol Moore, member of Committee for Waco Justice:
[http://serendipity.magnet.ch/waco/moore4.html]

Seventh Day Adventist Website:
[http://www.adventist.org]

FBI Website:
[http://www.fbi.gov]

Index

Index

Index

Picture Credits

MARYLOU MORANO KJELLE is a freelance writer and photojournalist who lives and works in Central New Jersey. Marylou writes a column for the *Westfield Leader/Times of Scotch Plains* called the "Children's Book Nook," where she reviews children's books and writes about the love of reading. *The Waco Siege* is her first book for Chelsea House Publishers.

JILL McCAFFREY has served for four years as national chairman of the Armed Forces Emergency Services of the American Red Cross. Ms. McCaffrey also serves on the board of directors for Knollwood—the Army Distaff Hall. The former Jill Ann Faulkner, a Massachusetts native, is the wife of Barry R. McCaffrey, who served in President Bill Clinton's cabinet as director of the White House Office of National Drug Control Policy. The McCaffreys are the parents of three grown children: Sean, a major in the U.S. Army; Tara, an intensive care nurse and captain in the National Guard; and Amy, a seventh grade teacher. The McCaffreys also have two grandchildren, Michael and Jack.